Raising Children Unto the Lord

Helping children build
a strong foundation in Christ

Lori Joiner

Blessings!
Lori Joiner
Gal 2:20

Lori Joiner
MINISTRIES

ISBN: 978-1-7325588-4-7

Cover Design by Andre Echevarria

Cover photo by Cassidy James Blaede on Unsplash

Back cover headshot by Evan Hadley

Interior design by Lisa Bell, Radical Women

Library of Congress Cataloging-in-Publication Data Joiner, Lori, 1972-

Raising Children Unto the Lord / Lori Joiner

Includes bibliographical references

Printed in the United States of America.

Dedication

I dedicate this book to two important men in my life.

THE first dedication is to my husband, Alan. Parenting is a two-person job. I will always be grateful to have a godly husband with whom to raise our sons. My ultimate prayer is for our sons take the best of you and the best of me and far surpass our wildest dreams for their lives. Alan, one of my favorite memories is of you tirelessly walking infant Josh around and around the house at 3:00 a.m. when he was colicky and would not stop crying unless he was being held and walked! Thank you for jumping in as a parent, bringing such stability to our lives and for driving the Joiner train.

Also, my father, Don Fleener. He has taught me to talk to anyone and everyone without prejudice. He never met a stranger and will talk to and respect all people in any position or station in life. This example has shaped my life in profound ways. Dad, I will always be so grateful for your belief in me over the years. No matter what my dream (to be an actress, to be a broadcaster, to be a spokesperson) you cheered me on without fail. I plan to pay this love, belief in, and pride forward to my sons in their lives the way you have done in mine.

Contents

Acknowledgments

THERE is no way this book would be in your hands without the love, grace and mercy of Almighty God. He created me, bought me with His blood and redeemed my wayward life unto Himself. He is my everything. He is my Lord and Savior, and I live for Him. He is the perfect Father who has given us the perfect parenting book, the Bible. Thank you, Lord, for all you have done in and through me for your glory.

I want to thank Ashley Cranefield for her early work in compiling this manuscript from my podcast notes. Thank you, Ashley for your dedicated work on this project. You are a joy to work with. Also, a special thank you to Gina Cranefield. Your keen eye to find mistakes, do preliminary editing work and help me get this manuscript to a form I could work with quickly is such a blessing. I am so thankful God crossed our paths so many years ago.

Finally, to my editor, Sandra Walters, I am grateful for your tireless work on this project. Thank you for believing in this work from a heart level, seeing what it could be, and guiding me and this book in a good direction. Your eye to see what was missing and your patience to bring me around to see it myself is a gift. Only God on His throne saw what we see now, a friendship and partnership for His glory!

Preface

EACH parent wants the best for their children. We desire to see them far outrun us in every area of life, whether that be with health, happiness, vitality, fruitfulness, finances, career or love for God! We dream of them reaching their full potential and being all they were created to be in Christ, but dreaming and hoping will only help our children just so much. We need to do more by having a plan, setting goals and having ideas to implement.

The Bible is our guide in all things in life, and especially with children. God makes this clear to us how to pass along our Christian hopes and dreams to our children and the generations that come after them. When we raise our children unto the Lord, we are not only helping them gain sure footing in Christ but helping their children and their children flourish for Christ down through the years. We must be intentional now to ensure a godly down-line later.

This book started as a podcast in 2022. I had just finished two seasons of *Your Discipleship Coach* podcast, where I spoke at length one episode after another episode about how to disciple women unto Christ. I decided to take a small detour for season three and thus did an entire series entitled *Your Discipleship Coach Kids Edition*. You are now holding the compilation of those episodes. You can certainly go back and listen to them firsthand to hear my voice, laughter, inflections and even tears in some episodes. As well as, now you can also have it compiled into what I hope is a helpful guide as you raise your children unto the Lord.

This parenting role is glorious and heart wrenching, exhilarating and exhausting all in one! It is scary and takes a huge reliance on the Holy Spirit to navigate new situations daily. I certainly don't think I have it all together and often wake up in the middle of the night concerned about my children, my parenting or something I did that day I should have done differently. However, I am prayerful, seeking God and trying to walk by faith in this wonderful, roller coaster job of parenting!

In Christ, Lori

Introduction

I recall sitting on the bench in our neighborhood playground when a friend asked, "Lori, how do you teach your children about God?" I was surprised at this question because this was a church-going mom. But it turns out, as I would later understand, many people are faithful in taking their kids to church to learn about God, but He is not actually being discussed in their homes. She wanted practical information-exactly what was I doing and when to teach my children about God at home.

I began to share with her some of the things I was doing to raise up my two most important disciples, my sons, in the Lord at home. One of the most important things I shared with her was how our children's spiritual maturity was primarily in the hands of parents. We need to take ownership of their spiritual growth. The Bible teaches this as well.

Deuteronomy 6:4-7

> 4 Hear, O Israel: The Lord our God, the Lord is
> one. 5 Love the Lord your God with all your
> heart and with all your soul and with all your
> strength. 6 These commandments that I give
> you today are to be on your hearts. 7 Impress
> them on your children. Talk about them when
> you sit at home and when you walk along the
> road, when you lie down and when you get up.

Learning about God and growing in God is supposed to be primarily taught in the home. The church serves as another great community to help in this endeavor, but the primary responsibility lies in the hands and hearts of parents. I would also add grandparents as well. Godly grandparents helping to pass along faith in Christ to future generations is such a bonus if you are blessed to have them in your life.

We cannot and should not leave raising our children unto the Lord to a Christian camp once a year during the summer, to the overworked youth director at the church or simply hoping they will pick something up at church on Sunday mornings. While all those activities are fine to layer into your child's life, you are the parent. You are the one talking with your children about God when you sit at home, when you walk along, when you lie down and when you get up. God needs to be a part of everyday life, not just life on Sunday mornings.

Don't feel overwhelmed or shut down because you feel as if you don't have what it takes to lead your children spiritually. You have what it takes by the simple fact you are holding this book. This proves to me you desire to make a difference for Christ in the lives of your children. Hang in there! The ideas in these pages are practical and will help you get the ball rolling!

Chapter 1

My Story and My Why

RAISING children unto the Lord is my passion because this was not my personal experience growing up as a child. As I reflect on my life, I think about how different my upbringing could have been if Christ had been the center of our home.

My parents met in college, married in college and gave birth to me when they were both still students at Oklahoma University. They later conceived two more children, three little girls in total. My father worked as a waiter in a restaurant, and my mother later finished school attaining her teaching degree.

My childhood became especially challenging because my parents drank and smoked marijuana. They even grew marijuana in our garden and dried it in my closet. During my early years, I recall fights, yelling and screaming, violence, broken objects and much childhood fear. After many years of this, my parents divorced when I was in the third grade, but things did not get better. The alcoholism followed them into their future marriages and so did the dysfunction.

There are countless times of terrifying situations that happened in our house. However, the one that stands out among others was one night when we were scared for our lives while my mom and her boyfriend drank and kept fighting through the night. My sister and I hid in our yard behind the doghouse as we waited for our mother's abusive boyfriend to leave. He finally drove off after what seemed like hours, and we wearily headed back into the house to fall asleep. We were shaken for days by this incident, and of course, I have never forgotten it.

During these growing-up years of turmoil, my mother taught me the Lord's prayer from the Bible, and she emphasized not saying the Lord's name in vain. She took us to church sporadically. When the pastor said something she did not like, we moved on to another church. I didn't attend any type of Sunday school, so church was totally boring to me. I languished on the pews coloring, waiting for the sermon to be over. It never seemed anything that was taught in church ever made it to our home in any type of functional way.

However, I am so thankful for my grandparents, who helped lend some stability to my life at that stage. We often spent the night with my grandparents, and they fed us in the evenings when we all went to the local cafeteria. My grandmother even enrolled us in dance lessons. One year, when it was bone chilling cold, they bought me a new coat as my mother neglected to see I needed one that fit.

Eventually, in the 8th grade, I left my mother to go live with my father in Texas. I hoped for a more stable environment. My father was a hard worker but addicted to alcohol and three packs of cigarettes a day. He and my stepmom, Nonie, did not attend church at all, not even on Christmas or Easter. There were no prayers, no Bible in the home, nothing that pointed to Christ. Thankfully, my stepmother was not an alcoholic, so while that home was far from perfect, it did provide more stability than life in Oklahoma.

When I lived with my father, he owned a restaurant in a small East Texas town named Carthage. We lived in a trailer, and both my dad and Nonie worked hard to make the restaurant a success. My stepmother entered me into a beauty pageant that summer to meet other girls, so I would have friends when the year began. And shockingly to us all, I won Junior Miss Panola County. I knew no one there and now had just won a pageant and sadly began to live a double life.

My dad and I celebrating after the pageant.

On the outside, I was a beauty queen, had taken dance and ballet my entire life thanks to my Oklahoma grandparents, so I displayed good stage presence and carried myself well. I made decent grades and even thought I was a Christian because I knew the Lord's prayer, did not say God's name in vain and attended church occasionally. However, I began to associate with a crowd of friends who would point me in the worst direction possible.

It seems no influences in my life were Christian. My friends were heavy drinkers, promiscuous, thieves and rebellious. I followed right along, with no road signs to live any differently. I began to drink and party and stayed in trouble in school. I was a follower wanting to please and be like my other partying friends. I wore my crown on top of my head during the Christmas parade. Then, I stayed out all weekend, never returning home, partying with my friends and lying to my parents. Finally, things went from bad to worse.

At age 15, my friend, Tina and I snuck out her father's truck one evening while her parents were gone. Neither of us possessed a license and decided to go for a joy ride around town. As we looked at the gas gage, it read: E, so we immediately went to the gas station. However, we could not even figure out how to get the gas cap off when we arrived. We had to ask a man pumping his gas to help us while Tina paid cash for the gas. I thank God to this day we did not die or kill someone else out on the road. We got home safely, but her sister told on us. Therefore, we thought we were doomed. The next day, Tina brought her mother's prescription Valium to school. We took some to "calm our nerves," and I passed out in class. I had never taken anything that strong before. Tina immediately confessed to giving me the pills and after going to the nurse, I was sent to the principal's office.

Once the principal found out the details of me taking prescription drugs at school, I was promptly told I would attend alternative school for 5 weeks. My history consisted of being in trouble often anyway for talking back to teachers, wearing too short miniskirts and more, so this was the straw that broke the camel's back. For 5 weeks, I went to alternative school instead of regular school. Sadly after 5 weeks, this did not get my attention. I was even more rebellious and partied just as hard afterward.

One of my other 15-year-old friends got a hardship license, and her father bought her a white Pontiac Firebird with red interior. I can still see it. We thought we looked so cool as we reclined in the seats, traveling down the streets. As I headed down a spiral of epic proportions, God was only in my life as a vacuum cleaner. When I made a big mess and was about to get in big trouble, I prayed to God. I asked Him to clean up my problem, get me out of a jam, help me conceal my secrets and make everything okay. I made deals with Him, but never kept up my end of the bargain, of course.

I recall being at an outdoor concert when two people tried to share the gospel with me and talk to me about Jesus. I told them about going to church as a young girl, how I prayed and how I knew the Lord's prayer. I was so prideful; I would not even hear them out. God threw me a lifeline, but my double life, my sin and rebellion, blinded me. Then, a dramatic shift happened.

We moved.

The summer after my sophomore year in high school, we moved to Houston. I went from a small town of 3,000 people to Houston, the fourth largest city in America, with over 2 million people. I left the summer before my junior year of high school. I thought this was probably the worst thing that could happen to me, having to move, but it actually turned out to be one of the best things for me.

We moved to a neighborhood with lots of kids my age. The Powell family lived a few houses down, and their kids who were my age invited me to their church. I went because I had no friends in this big city, and I, funny enough, still thought of myself as a Christian. When I compared myself to others doing drugs, going to jail and smoking, etc., I figured I was better than them. I based my salvation at that point in me being just slightly better than others.

I had a good experience when attending church with the Powell family and decided I would go back. There are two main reasons for this decision to return to church. One, there were cute guys in the youth group, and two, there were plenty of doughnuts to eat. So, each week that summer, I got up on Sunday mornings, joined them for church, ate the doughnuts and would sometimes even go with them afterwards to Luby's cafeteria for lunch. The youth director and his wife were exceptionally kind people whom I enjoyed being around. Sadly, though, I started my junior year of high school and began to return to my old ways.

I met a high school dropout who raced cars illegally, drank and smoked, and I decided to date him. Then, my double life started back up again. Friday and Saturday nights I hung out with him, racing cars, using the money for alcohol and food, going to dance clubs, drinking and partying. When Sunday morning rolled around, I attended church with the Powells, eating doughnuts, flirting with the boys and going to lunch at Luby's as usual. I even went on Sunday nights with the Powells, as they had Sunday night activities for youth.

One evening, the youth director of this church asked to speak with me following the service. I thought, *Is he going to scold me for passing notes in church?* While I attended church regularly, I understood very little of the words being said or taught. So, I often passed the time by writing notes to my friends, asking where we were going afterward and who I would ride with. This evening though, I felt my rebellious nature rising, and I would not stand for his correction. I decided if he corrected me; I would stop coming all together. My parents did not care if I went to church or not, so it would be no big deal for me to totally drop this from my life. Thankfully, he delivered a different message to me that evening.

All the kids left for Burger King, and I sat on one of the pews in the church while he spoke to me one-on-one with his wife just around the corner. Instead of scolding me for the note passing, he explained kindly how much God loved me. He shared God not only loved me but also had a plan for my life. "Lori, you are not a coincidence of life. God has a purpose for you," he said. He further explained because of sin in my life, I was separated from God's love and plan and how my sin had built a wall between God and me. No one had to convince me I was a sinner. I knew this for a fact. I just did not think I was that bad. I had been to alternative school, lived a promiscuous lifestyle, drank, etc., but when I compared myself to others, I always came out on top in my mind. The sliding scale I used to determine my eternal destiny always showed me on top.

He told me of Jesus dying on the cross for my sins. John 3:16 in the Bible says, "For God so loved the world that he gave his one and only Son, that whoever believes in him shall not perish but have eternal life."

He further shared how Jesus had died for me, in my place, and then rose again three days later. He explained it was not my goodness or badness that determined my eternal destiny, but Jesus' death on my behalf and my faith in Him and His sacrifice for me. Something in my heart melted as he spoke. I now know this was the Holy Spirit making me alive spiritually, convicting me of my sins and showing me clearly the choice I had to make. Would I trust in my "good works" or being a relatively "good person," or would I place my faith in Jesus Christ and His death on my behalf, His burial and resurrection which gives new life to all who believe? The fork in the road was before me. My heart was trembling. Would I continue my rebellious ways, following in the footsteps of my parents and my partying friends, or would I turn my life over to God?

Tears began to stream down my face. God was calling me to Himself and extending yet another lifeline. Black mascara slid down my cheeks with each tear. That night of October 1988, I got on my knees and talked to God. This time, instead of asking Him to clean up a particular mess I had gotten myself into, I surrendered myself to Him. I prayed and asked Jesus to forgive me of my sins and to come into my heart as my Lord and Savior. I thanked Him for the gift of eternal life in Heaven with Him based on Jesus, not on my works. I also asked Him to make me the person He meant for me to be. At that moment, I became born again. I was not simply His creation but now His child in the faith, and He was my heavenly Father. The youth director later gave me a Bible and a booklet where I learned how to spend time with God each day. He also gave me a notebook and taught me how to listen to the sermons on Sunday mornings while taking notes as the pastor taught. All seemed to be going well, but my double life caught up with me.

I was late. I thought, *Am I pregnant?*

When the realization hit me that I may be carrying a baby, I became so sad. I wanted to attend in order to grow in my relationship with Jesus and really get involved in the youth group for the right reasons. Instead, I called my boyfriend, and we talked about us possibly getting married and moving into his parents' house.

I remember sitting in his race car bawling. He did not understand my other life. The life where I placed my faith in Jesus, and God rescued me from hell and how I was born again. He had nothing against me going to church, but we simply lived in two different worlds. It was something I did with my neighbors on Sundays.

Our youth group planned on going to a conference, so I decided to go as well. While attending, I was utterly distracted the entire time. I grieved how this church stuff would be over. It may not have been over, but in my 16-year-old mind, I thought, *This will all be coming to an end soon.* I had been living a double life, and the life I tried to leave behind somehow had taken over. I could not concentrate, but I remember a time in the conference where you could pray with a youth counselor. I imagined kids talking to the counselors about strict parents, bad grades, peer pressure of some sort, but not me. When the youth counselor at the conference walked over to me, I said, "I think I am pregnant!" I do not even remember what he said, but I am sure he was not ready for that shocker of a confession. I had enough of dealing with the double life. I wanted to live for God, but I felt I was hanging on by a thread.

On the way home from the conference on the last day, our youth group stopped at McDonald's for dinner. I used the restroom, and there I realized I was NOT pregnant. I cried in that bathroom stall. So many emotions were flooding through my heart, my eyes and my body.

I broke up with the boyfriend later that night on the phone. He understood, and I never saw him again. To say I threw myself into my youth group and God would be a total understatement. I went ALL IN FOR JESUS and frankly have never looked back. My youth director discipled me and taught me how to spend time with God, how to share Christ with other people and how to make unpopular stands for Christ. My youth director would take us to the Galleria Mall in downtown Houston, and he trained us to walk up to people in the food court and share the gospel with them. I remember the first night I approached a girl my age eating dinner in the food court. I asked her if I could share with her how to get to heaven. We had a lengthy conversation and after I explained what Jesus had done for us, she also surrendered her life to Christ. Witnessing another person place their faith in the Lord was such a joy.

God had not only rescued me and saved me, but He was now using me for His glory! He had a purpose for my life, to be a women's minister, an author, a disciple maker, and I could not be happier. In my office hangs a sign which reads, "Begin each day with a grateful heart." When I recall the dead-end road I was on in high school, I am filled overflowing with gratefulness and thankfulness to Him.

Jesus has since become my best friend. He has been the most faithful, loving Lord. I often think of a scripture in the book of Psalm 40:2, which says, "He lifted me out of the slimy pit, out of the mud and mire; he set my feet on a rock and gave me a firm place to stand." Through the ups and downs in life, He has been with me, guiding me through, and I now live to fall deeper in love with Him and tell others about Him.

Not only do I love ministering to women, helping them come to know and grow in Christ, but I now see my two sons as my main disciples. I 100% want them to have a different life and childhood than I had. From day one I taught them how God loves them, has a purpose for their lives and how God's Word is our roadmap in life. In the Bible, God teaches us how to stay on the narrow path instead of the wide path which leads to destruction. I know that path well, and I'm training my children to recognize and stay away from it. I cannot control all their decisions. However, I can at least do my best to point them to Christ and train them in the Lord. It is a bit of a risk to write about parenting when my children have yet to leave my nest, but I feel a calling, a burden and a stewardship to at least share what I have done until now in their upbringing. I am not a perfect mother. I have my own regrets and mommy guilt and many instances where I wish I could have a do-over. I pray God would use me in their lives, though. My sons are God's children, on loan to me in a way. And I have an incredible responsibility to protect them provide for them and point them to Christ.

I have taught them both that it is not their career, college or their grades that matter most in life. It is walking with God, pleasing Him and fulfilling the purpose for which He created them.

I pray this for your family as well. That you are able to learn from your childhood, whether good or bad, and make the changes needed to guide your children to the Lord, to pray for them to be mighty in His kingdom and see them fulfill their God given destiny for His glory!

We are in this together. With God on our side, in our hearts and leading us by His Word, there is nothing He can't do in and through us and our children!

Chapter 2

Pray Out Loud with Your Children

ONE afternoon, over lunch, a friend and I discussed our most recent parenting experiences. She told me during our talk that despite her family's involvement in the church, her children had never heard her pray out loud. I couldn't believe it. Her kids were older. One was in junior high, the other in elementary school. As we talked further, she admitted she absolutely disliked praying out loud. Her children hadn't seen or heard her pray. She had avoided praying with her children for so long she was now unsure how to even start.

Praying out loud with your children is key in raising them unto the Lord. In this chapter, we will explore *why* to pray out loud, *what* to pray out loud, *when* to pray and tips for *getting started* if this has not been your regular practice at home.

There are numerous reasons to pray out loud over your children, or you could say with your children each day. Here are the top three reasons I pray out loud with my sons each day and have since they were infants.

When I pray out loud with my children, I am modeling for them *how* to pray.

Prayer is simply talking to God. When I pray, they hear me talking to God. I do not use any fancy language when I pray or fancy words I would not use in regular dialogue with another person. When I pray, I do not beg

God for things or only ask for things. They hear me praise God for being a good God, an all-knowing God, a loving God. They hear me ask God for souls to be saved, people to be healed and for their protection.

Just as I taught them how to fold their clothes by modeling how to fold various items, and I showed them where to put each piece of silverware as I took it out of the dishwasher, I modeled prayer as well. In addition, their father demonstrated how to mow the grass by teaching how to start the lawnmower, how to steer and how to dispose of the clippings appropriately. Prayer modeling is no different.

They must observe and hear us praying as role models. They learn how to pray to God, just as they learn how to cut the lawn, put the dishes away and fold their clothes, by hearing it modeled. So, why would we not model prayer like everything else? I am not leaving it up to my friends to show my kids how to fold clothes or mow the lawn. I will also not leave it to the church to teach them how to pray. It is my responsibility and by modeling it we do our children and grandchildren a huge favor and service for their future spiritual lives.

When I pray out loud with my children, I am teaching them *what* they can pray for.

When I pray with my sons, they hear me ask God for big things and little things. They have been taught no item is too big, and no item is too small to ask God for help. For example, together with my sons, we have prayed for them to do well on an upcoming test or quiz, for God to aid them in remembering what they have learned, for their friends to trust Christ as Savior and Lord and for sicknesses to go away.

One time, my son left his iPad at a basketball game. We arrived home, changed our clothes and prepared to get into bed when he realized it was left at school. We jumped back into the car, and as I drove, he and I prayed for the iPad to be exactly where he left it. And sure enough, the device was! God protected his iPad from being stolen that night. We have prayed to feel better, to resolve friend drama and for teachers.

I have been in ministry for over 30 years, and at times, women I am discipling will say to me, "I am not sure I can pray for that." So many people are insecure about what items can be brought to God in prayer. They think either an item concerning them is too big for God to deal with or too insignificant for God to care about. Or they feel an issue they are concerned about may or may not be God's will, so they are unsure how to pray.

I taught my children through praying out loud with them. Therefore, they know they can pray for *ANYTHING*, and God will sort it out. Big things like healing for sick people, small things like an iPad and confusing things we are not sure how to pray about. They have heard me give things to God and trust His will. Mamas and Dads please let your children hear your prayers. They need to know they can pray for *ANYTHING*.

When I pray out loud with my children, they hear what I am praying for them *personally*.

As they hear me specifically pray for them, it helps to form their inner godly identity. Here is a sample prayer I pray over Josh and Jake each day. I simply wrote what I could remember from my prayer for them this morning. I prayed,

"Dear Lord, I pray you would give Josh a great day at school today. I pray you would give Josh a long life and the ability to lay up much treasure in heaven. Please help him be a man after your own heart. I pray blessings and favor would chase him down today and all his days.

Please protect Josh from sickness, illness, disease, accidents and calamity. I pray he would be a leader, not a follower. That even if everyone else is doing something wrong, Josh would have the self-control and leadership to do what is right. I pray he would be an example of what a godly man looks like.

Thank you that you made Josh a Joiner! Thank you for putting him in our family and letting me be his mommy! Father, you say that your sheep hear your voice. Josh is one of your sheep-please help him learn to hear your voice clearly and walk with you daily.

I pray Josh would be a mighty man in your kingdom. I pray he would have a heart that seeks hard after you. Father, please surround Josh with your angels today and protect him against all odds. Please guard his heart, his mind and his body today. Please give him the mind of Christ, the heart of Christ and the feet of Christ. Lord, keep Josh on the narrow road. Please bind his feet to paths of righteousness.

Lord, please bring Josh safely home to his pillow tonight. Amen."

Josh is hearing how I desire for God to make him a leader, that he would have an eternal mindset and for God to help him lay up treasure in heaven. Think about how this may play out in his life. He has heard me pray hundreds of times for him to be a leader. Then, the moment comes at some point for him to take a stand or actually lead, and he knows this is what he is supposed to do. No matter how fearful he might be. He is aware he has a storehouse of years of prayers built up for him in this area.

I pray out loud for him to be able to hear God's voice and direction in his life, so when he feels God leading or directing him, he does not need to doubt. He KNOWS this has been prayed over him hundreds of times. Regardless of how fearful he may be to take a scary step of faith, he will be able to do it knowing he is hearing from God Almighty.

I pray this or something like this, each and every day. I am not only praying for him, but modeling how to pray and what to pray for. In addition, I am speaking in faith what I want to be true of him. When he is not with me and on his own, he can hear God's voice and follow it. He can say to himself, "I am a leader. What would a godly leader do?" And act in faith.

When to pray for your children

I pray in the morning when I wake my kids up for school. As they are lying in their beds, I come in, sit on the side of their beds, rub their backs to wake them up and begin to speak out loud a prayer such as the one I outlined for you. If they have woken up on their own, I give them a hug, and as I stand there hugging them, I am praying over them out loud. My husband and I also pray with each child at night before bedtime. My husband always thanks God for bringing them home safely to their pillows at night, for God to forgive their sins and cover them with the blood of Jesus. They are not simply hearing *my* prayers for them, but also their dad's prayers, which I think is so important as well. If at all possible, both parents should regularly pray over their children.

I pray in the mornings, but my husband is already at work by the time our children wake up, which is why he doesn't pray with them in the mornings. We both pray out loud for our sons before bedtime each night, and of course, we pray anytime during the day if needed.

I recall one afternoon a neighbor of mine being discharged from the hospital. Despite being in such poor health, she was nonetheless released. As she dealt with a long road of rehabilitation and agony ahead, I desired to support and pray for her, so I made the decision to go with my younger son, Jake. She had a kidney condition, and it wasn't contagious. Therefore, I felt okay taking him. We also took our new miniature dachshund, Hershey, with us because she adorned this little puppy.

I explained to Jake we would be praying for her while we were there. Then, we headed over to our neighbor's house with the dog in-tow. We chatted with her as she patted Hershey on the head, and then we prayed. Jake folded his little 8-year-old hands and prayed for her to be healed from her sickness. My point here is that we pray for others too, not just in the morning or at night. Prayer is a part of our lives as a family. By the way, she recovered from the illness.

She still remembers how comforting it was to hear his little voice praying for her and see his tiny hands folded in prayer many years later. Jake's prayer really touched my neighbor.

To reiterate, Jake knew how to pray and what to pray for because he had heard me modeling to him over and over and over throughout the years. He believes God can heal people, not because he has heard me ask God to heal others, but he has also seen the results of his prayers.

Finally, what if you are not in the habit of doing this?

What if you were not taught this or have never experienced someone modeling prayer for you and feel nervous praying in front of others? Or perhaps, you believe your kids will think you have lost your mind if you all of a sudden begin to pray out loud for them. Let me share some advice here.

First, no one ever prayed over me like this, either. I do recall my mom teaching me to pray the Lord's prayer at night. That is the prayer found in Luke chapter 11, where Jesus teaches his disciples to pray. It begins with, "Our Father, who is in heaven, hallowed be thy name…" and we would pray this out loud together in the evenings, so I am thankful for that. These types of prayers I pray with my kids were never modeled to me. However, this does not hold me back from praying with my children, so please do not let it hold you back, either. It is never too late to start a new great habit.

If you have never done this, then start really, really small. As your child wakes up tomorrow morning, give them a hug and say, "Lord, thank you that this kid is my kid!" And then look them in the eyes and say, "I love you, and I am so glad God gave you to me!"

The next day as they are leaving for school, give them a hug, and squeeze them while saying, "Lord please protect ________ today and bring him or her home safely!"

Look your child in the eyes and say, "I wish I would have been praying over you like this each day of your life, but better late than never!"

Over time, you can pray for them at night at their bedside, at a meal or for an upcoming test they are studying for. Eventually, it will be natural to pray for them, and they will come to understand this is simply how things are now.

It is not too late, my friends. I never heard my dad pray until after he was 54 years old. He placed his faith in Christ around that time and began to grow in his faith. It has been amazing to see his life transform for God. He now plays guitar in the church band. I was a grown woman in my 30s living on my own when he first started praying for me. And now I love when he prays for me out loud, usually as we are starting a meal or as he is leaving to go back home after a visit. So, it is not too late for you to start praying out loud for your kids, even your adult children.

I am thrilled to hear him pray and to know my dad is praying for me and my family. So please, even if your kids are older and this is new to you, start now!

Here is another idea to help you get started praying for your kids. Say to your children while holding this book in your hands, "I read a book recently about how important it is to pray out loud with your children. I know I have not done this ever, or on a regular basis, but I have always prayed for you in my head and in my heart. Now, I want you to hear what I am praying for, so starting today, I am going to let you in on what I ask God for you each day." And then go for it!

Lori sitting on her father's lap.

You can start today even if you have never done this. Some people haven't run a marathon before, but they decide to do so. They get off the couch, train for it and cross the finish line! Others have never snow skied, but they make the drive to the slopes, perhaps take a class and off they go down the greens and blues. Some people have never painted a house before, but they watch a few YouTube tutorials, and voila, a new coat of paint. Some people have never prayed out loud over their children or grandchildren before, but guess what? You can start today, like you would start any new activity or habit.

Each year, I like to choose a verse of scripture to pray over my children as the school year starts. This year, I chose–

Luke 2:40 "There the child grew up healthy and strong. He was filled with wisdom, and God's favor was on him."

This verse described Jesus as a young boy, but I wrote this verse down on an index card and prayed it out loud over Josh and Jake. Why don't you do that as well? Take this verse, or any verse you find as you read scripture and say to your children, "I found this verse in scripture this morning as I was reading, and it emulates what I want to be true in your lives. Please pray with me as I pray this for you." Then, all of you can bow your heads and you can say this verse along with anything else you may want to add in prayer.

The Bottom Line

Your children, at any age from infancy to adulthood, will benefit greatly to hear you pray over them out loud. I pray for my sons countless times throughout the day. When they are with me, I pray out loud, so I can model to them that they can ask God for anything. They can talk to God like they talk to me. By praying out loud, they can hear what I am praying for them personally. By praying out loud, I am discipling them to be more like Christ as we read of Christ praying for things all through scripture and guess what? He prayed out loud!

Chapter 3

Help Your Children Read the Bible

READING the Bible to our kids is one of the main ways they discover who God is. The Bible is the primary source of information when it comes to raising our kids unto the Lord. The Bible gives examples of God's personality, grace, love, mercy, hatred of sin and pardon for sin. We need to read the Bible to young children and pass along the lessons we learn to them. We are doing this in accordance with Moses' advice to the Israelite people in the Old Testament.

> **Deuteronomy 6:6-7**
> 6 These commandments that I give you today are to
> be on your hearts. 7 Impress them on your children.
> Talk about them when you sit at home and when you walk along the road, when you lie down and when you get up.

We are to teach them God's commandments, stories about God and basic biblical knowledge and help. Eventually, when our children begin to read, they can slowly be guided to read the Bible themselves. Teaching your children to read the Bible or a biblical devotional daily will greatly benefit their spiritual maturity over the years.

I understand many families are very busy with multiple children and various ages and stages of life. Perhaps the thought of adding in Bible reading to your already full to-do-list is making you feel overwhelmed. Hang in there! Daily Bible reading can be accomplished during something you may already be doing. It won't add to the list of things to do but perhaps replace or enhance something already on the schedule.

Three reasons to open the Bible or at least a Bible devotional each day:

1. **The Bible is the primary way God speaks to us as humans.**

God wants to communicate with us, and He speaks to us through scripture. The words on the pages of the Bible can help us when we are tempted, can comfort us when we are sad and direct us when we have decisions to face. God uses His Word in our lives daily, actively and consistently. We communicate with God through prayer, but God does not pray to us. He uses His word to speak to us. Knowing how God communicates with us is vitally important in helping our children establish a time in their daily lives to actually read God's Word.

2. **The Bible is filled with examples of what to do and examples of what not to do.**

Explaining to our children right from wrong is a pivotal role in the life of a parent. Backing up this teaching with examples from real life will enhance these lessons further. I have taught my boys they can learn from the lives of everyone presented in scripture. They will learn what to do to stay in step with God's plan for their lives and examples of people who did not stay in step with God's plan and the sad consequences.

My older son was reading about King Saul last week. He read of Saul's jealousy over David, how he literally went insane at the end of his life and then killed himself on his own sword. We talked about how Saul's story could have ended differently had Saul obeyed God at each step of his life and kingship. Instead, Saul cut his own life short and thus canceled any further opportunity to lay up treasure in heaven. Even the worst example of a person's life in scripture can be used as teachable moments in your kids' lives. And of course, there are plenty of great examples of faith and trust in God as well throughout scripture.

3. **Reading the Bible daily will help your child spiritually for a lifetime.**

All parents teach their children good habits when they are young. Take, for example, teaching children to brush their teeth. When kids are young, they have no concept for why they need to brush their teeth. They see it as a chore and can't really understand the long-term benefits. However, as the adult, you teach this, nonetheless. You teach them to brush in small circles, to get the gums and tongue and to always use toothpaste, etc. Why? Because you know better than they do. You know how important it is to establish good hygiene as a habit early, so they can save themselves years of pain and expense on their teeth. Further, you are teaching them to wear a helmet while riding their bike, teaching them safety in the sun by wearing sunscreen, safety as a new driver and so on. These habits will help them now and set them up for success later.

As the parent, you must help them establish these habits. For example, brushing teeth, showering regularly, wearing a seatbelt, daily Bible reading is no different. Helping your child establish a regular time when they are learning from God through scripture about Jesus, the Holy Spirit, how to say no to temptation and yes to righteousness, are only a few of the many incredible lessons found in the Bible. Reading daily, learning from the Word, applying scriptures to their lives will help them now and in the future. The largest benefits will be reaped in heaven one day.

Tips to help establish a daily time of Bible reading:

Choose a time in the day to read the Bible and then put this activity on autopilot! Once you establish the habit, this won't seem like another thing to check off your list. For me, I chose mornings for my sons. Breakfast time turned out to be our sweet spot for us to read our Bible or devotionals.

Toddler Years: When my boys were toddlers, they would each have a turn sitting in my lap in the mornings as they drank juice from their sippy cups. I would read to them from a children's devotional book. The one I used is named The Beginner's Bible, Kids Sized Devotions published by Zonderkidz. The pages had a lot of white space. The characters were cartoon drawings, and the teachings were simple. I would read one short devotion each morning. Like I mentioned, my sons were little, and I am sure half of what I was saying and reading to them they could not even comprehend. This time lasted 3 to 5 minutes, tops.

During this short time in the mornings, they began to hear words, names and places written in the Bible. At the most basic level, they were just easing into the habit of sitting still for 3-5 minutes and listening to me read a biblical devotional while they looked at a picture.

Of course, as your kids begin to read, they can read along with you. They will find words and short phrases they can read back to you. For example, I would point to words and ask questions like these:

"Josh, what is this word?" I asked.

"God," he responded.

I then replied, "Yes! Now, what does this say?"

He would respond, "God loves me."

To which I would reply, "Yes!"

You can do the same kids devotional year after year because let's face it, they did not pick up much the first time through or even the next year. However, you started the repetition, which is so key to children's learning. You established a time for God in the daily schedule.

Elementary Years: As my boys were growing and reading on their own, I got them each their own devotional, and they read as they ate breakfast before school. We don't watch cartoons or any TV in the mornings before school in the Joiner home. There are no electronics out, no iPads, no TV, in the mornings. This is a quiet time of reading devotionals.

As they eat their breakfast, they read. See, not another added thing on the to-do list. I simply let them eat and read at the same time. For this stage of life, I really liked the devotional titled Our Daily Bread for Kids: 365 Meaningful Moments with God published by Discovery House. These devotionals were simple enough for them to read on their own, but a bit lengthier and with an application to life.

Jake reading a devotional at breakfast.

Junior High Years: This year, my son is in the 6th grade and is reading The Purpose Driven Life: Devotional for Kids by Rick Warren. This is a normal book-sized devotional, which includes a verse or passage of scripture, a short story about the verse and how it can apply to a kid's life. There are no pictures like in his past devotionals.

He reads as well as applies the principles and verses to his life the best he can as a 12-year-old.

High School Years: My 9th grader is reading through the Bible using The One Year Bible. This is an excellent way to read the Bible as a high schooler or adult. It divides up the actual Bible into 365 daily readings. At this point, he does not want to read only one scripture per day as in a devotional but wants to read larger portions of the Bible and whole stories at a time. He told me yesterday he enjoys the One Year Bible because it includes passages from the Old Testament and New Testament each day. I love to hear what he is reading and what he thinks about it. We have many discussions after he reads each morning.

As I mentioned before, mornings at breakfast worked best for me to help my sons establish this daily habit of connecting with God through reading the Bible. I have no plans right now to change this purposeful practice in their lives. My kids are so firmly rooted in this devotional breakfast time; I pray this pattern follows them into adulthood.

Daytime or Nighttime Bible Reading May Work Better for Your Family.

I know one mom who reads the same Our Daily Bread for Kids devotional to her children out loud each night before bed. This is their established plan, and her children know their mom will read to them from a devotional or from the Bible each night.

Of course, there is an entire empire of home school families who are incorporating daily Bible reading into their day at some point, even including it into their actual schoolwork and learning. I know one homeschool mom that uses the mornings for walking the dog, chores and breakfast with her kids, then starts Bible reading time later in the afternoon.

The point is, and I want to stress this again, there is a plan in place. Typically, after about a month or so, this activity is on autopilot.

Be Intentional About Establishing a Daily Bible Reading Habit.

My children are in public school. They are without my godly influence in their lives for 7 hours a day. That is 35 hours a week. This is why I do not believe one or two hours a weekend at church is enough to stand up against any secular or anti-biblical views they may be facing at school. Bible reading and connecting with God through scripture needs to be a daily practice, not just a weekend practice.

If this has not been your routine to have a Bible time in your daily schedule, I want to encourage you to start now. Not next month, not next semester, don't put it off to the fall and the start of a new school year. Start now. It will NOT feel like another "To Do" in your schedule. As a matter of fact, this can bring peace.

One reason the mornings worked for us is because I found when we did not do Bible reading in the mornings, the start of the day became stressful. There was a season I can recall where we were watching cartoons. The boys would begin to fight over what cartoon to watch, who had the remote, get distracted watching cartoons and not eat their food. This resulted in me barking at them to "Eat! Eat! Finish up! Finish up!" Then, we would run late for the bus, and I would really be barking orders such as, "Hurry, get your shoes on! Hurry, grab your backpack!"

This was such a yucky way to begin the day for all of us, but reading God's Word, asking about what they read, even explaining things to them to help them understand and apply to their lives, is 100% more peaceful. The shift away from electronics to scripture is not only more peaceful, but they are learning and growing in their walk with God as they read. He communicates to them through what they read.

The Bottom Line

Intentionality is key to establishing this Bible reading habit. Examine your daily routine. What can be tweaked to make room for God to speak through His Word to your child? What can be deleted, moved or changed to make time for connecting to God through Bible reading? If you are at a loss, then take it to the Lord in prayer. Ask Him for guidance, wisdom, even bravery, to turn the ship in a new direction. I am rooting for you!

Chapter 4

Share the Gospel with Your Children

OUR children are our number one priority when it comes to discipleship. The Bible is clear: we are to make disciples of all nations, baptizing them and teaching them to obey all Jesus has commanded, and our first disciples are our children. We need to make sure we are passing on basic biblical truths and lessons which will not only help them in life but help them in eternity. The Bible exhorts parents to train up their children in the knowledge of the Lord, and we need to be great stewards of this responsibility.

So far, we have covered the importance of praying out loud with our children and grandchildren and setting up a daily Bible reading time, so our children can connect with God on their own on a regular basis. Our next step in raising our children unto the Lord is to clearly explain the gospel message to our kids, so they can place their personal faith in Christ.

Goals When Discipling our Children:

As we lead our children spiritually by praying over them, reading the Bible to them and helping them set up a time to read the Bible, we do this with a number of goals in mind.

1. **We are teaching them who God is.**

We want our children to know God is the Creator of the universe, the Savior of mankind, and He can live in each heart, directing them according to His plan for their lives. We teach them that God is 3 in 1: God the Father, God the Son and God the Holy Spirit. We explain that God stepped into history 2,000 years ago to die for the sins of humanity to reconcile us back to Himself.

2. **We want them to know they were created by a loving God.**

Our children are not a coincidence or here by chance. They have been created special and God breathed life into each of them on purpose. He has a destiny for them and each aspect of their body, such as hair color, eyes, gifts, talents and abilities, can be used by Him to advance the Great Commission and help them lay up treasure in Heaven.

3. **The number one goal, however, is for each child to personally place their faith in Jesus Christ.**

We must teach our children that in order for them to live in heaven for eternity with God, a relationship with Jesus needs to be established. Jesus lived a perfect life on earth and is the only sacrifice for sins. He died for our sins on the cross, was buried and rose from the grave three days later and has ascended to heaven. By placing our faith and trust in Jesus and receiving Him as Savior and Lord, we can know Him personally and live with Him eternally in Heaven. There are four main points of the gospel message. The gospel message is also referred to as the "Good News." So, I could say, here are the four main points of the good news or I could say the four main points of the gospel message–I am referring to the same four points either way.

Point number 1: God loves us.

John 3:16 "God so loved the world, that He gave His only begotten son, that whoever believes in him will not perish but have eternal life."

Point number 2: We are sinful.

Romans 3:23 "All have sinned and fall short of the glory of God."

Point number 3: Jesus Christ is God's only provision for man's sin. Through Him alone, we can know God personally and experience His love.

Romans 5:8 "God demonstrates His own love toward us, in that while we were yet sinners, Christ died for us."

1 Corinthians 15:3-6 "Christ died for our sins… He was buried…He was raised on the third day according to the scriptures…He appeared to Peter, then to the twelve. After that, he appeared to more than five hundred…"

John 14:6 "Jesus said to him, 'I am the way, the truth and the life; no one comes to the Father, but through me.'"

Point number 4: We must individually receive Jesus Christ as Savior and Lord; then we can know God personally and experience His love.

John 1:12 "As many as received Him, to them he gave the right to become children of God, even to those who believe in His name."

Ephesians 2:8-9 "By grace you have been saved through your faith; and that not of yourselves, it is a gift of God; not as a result of works that no one should boast."

We receive Christ by placing our faith in Christ through a personal invitation.

Christ said in Revelation 3:20, "Behold, I stand at the door and knock; if anyone hears my voice and opens the door, I will come into Him."

These are the four basic points of the Gospel or the Good News. This was the message given to me as a 16-year-old young woman by the youth director of a local church. And as I stated in chapter one, after this gospel message was explained to me, I sank to my knees and in prayer placed my faith in Jesus as my Lord and Savior.

I have been teaching my children the four main points of the gospel message since they were toddlers. Furthermore, I prayed they would make this decision at a young age, so that they could have Christ in their lives throughout junior high, high school and college. I am not simply leaving it to the church to ensure my children have heard and understand the gospel. This is my responsibility and your responsibility as the parent seeking the best for their child spiritually.

Understand, we cannot *make* a child, or any person, place their faith in Christ. We cannot pressure. We cannot guilt, and we cannot scare a person into placing faith in Christ. If we do, we will sabotage it! If a child or a person places their faith in Christ because they feel pressure from me–then it is not a genuine decision of faith. It was about me, not about Christ. It was about me–not about them surrendering their life and eternity to Christ. What we *can* do is present the gospel clearly, often with stories and with verses from the Bible.

How to share the gospel with your child and lead them to faith in Christ:

1. Share your story of salvation with your kids.

One of the ways I shared my salvation story with my children was to use a picture on my refrigerator. I was fortunate to visit the church where I placed my faith in Christ 20 years after I made that life-changing decision. I went to the very pew where I knelt down, as a wayward teenager, and asked Jesus Christ to come into my life, to forgive me of my sins and give me the gift of eternal life with Him. My husband took a picture of me seated on that pew. I later printed it out and placed it on my refrigerator at eye level of my two young sons.

Lori on the pew where she placed her faith in Christ.

Each time they looked at the picture, I reminded them of my story and how mommy placed her faith in Christ. I always told them how I was praying for them to one day make the same decision for Christ. As they grew older, the picture climbed the refrigerator to match their height. Often, we talked at length about what the gospel message is, how a person places their faith in Christ and how they can make the same decision.

2. Use nighttime prayers to reiterate the gospel.

One night, when Jake was five years old, we talked during his bedtime routine. He had been learning about the Easter story in church. I knew he had heard the gospel several times at church and with me. I asked him if he could tell me about Jesus and what Jesus did on the cross. He knew the story well. I told him that Jesus died on the cross for him personally! I further explained he could place his faith in Jesus and trust Christ for the forgiveness of his sins. I asked if he would like to pray to God, and he said, "Yes." He prayed in his own way to put his faith in Christ. Afterward, he held his Bible, and I took his picture. I wanted him to know, even as he got older, he had placed his faith in Christ, and I was there to hear it and even take a picture!

3. Ask your children if they can reiterate their salvation story to you.

When Josh was in the second or third grade, I remember asking him if he had made a decision to place his faith in Christ or if he would like to do that with me. He said, "I have already done that mom." I said, "Oh really? When was that?" He explained how he prayed to ask Jesus into his heart when the children's pastor asked the kids to pray with him if they wanted Jesus in their lives. I said, "Well, awesome buddy! I am proud of you for doing that." Then he added, "Yes, I now pray that same prayer each week when the pastor prays at church." I was able to use this as an opportunity to explain that once we place our faith in Christ, He is there and will never leave us. Hebrews 13:5 says, "Never will I leave you, never will I forsake you."

4. Use time in the car for spiritual conversations.

As my friend drove her junior high son home from church one evening, she asked, "Have you placed your faith in Christ? She wanted to know where he was spiritually. He responded that indeed he had accepted Christ as his Savior. With this information, she knew he was a follower of Christ and looked for ways to help him grow in Christ, such as getting plugged into a Bible study, attending church regularly and even opportunities to grow in Christ at school.

5. Use holidays to reiterate the gospel message.

When holidays roll around each year, especially Christmas and Easter, explain in detail what is being celebrated. For example, at Christmas explain we are celebrating the birth of Jesus Christ. Read from the Bible the actual story in Luke chapters 1 and 2. At Easter, explain we celebrate Jesus Christ who died for the sins of the world. He was buried and then raised from the dead three days later. And how now, we serve a risen Savior. You can further explain how Jesus lived a perfect life, willingly laid down His life and paid the penalty of our sins. By placing our faith in Him, one can have eternal life with God.

After any of the above scenarios, you can always share your story of placing your faith in Christ and simply ask if your child would like to do the same. If they say yes, then you can both pray together. If they say no, you can inquire as to why not.

Examples of salvation prayers:

We need to understand that when a person places their faith in God, it is not so much the exact words but the attitude of the heart. God is looking for faith, not a script. However, a simple prayer expressing faith is fine to convey to the Lord.

I personally have taught my sons this three-word prayer: *Sorry, Thank you, Please.* I rehearsed,

"Dear God, I am SORRY for my sins. THANK YOU that you love me, and you died for my sins. PLEASE come into my heart and life. I place my trust in you."

I taught this to my sons so that if they ever had a friend who wanted to place their faith in Christ, they could easily remember what to say to help them make that life-changing decision.

Have *you* had a *Sorry*, *Thank you, Please* moment with God? It is hard to pass on something you don't possess yourself. What a tragedy it would be to teach your children about faith in Christ but miss the boat yourself. If you cannot pinpoint a time and place where you surrendered your life to Christ, don't put that decision off. Think: What is the basis of your own faith? If you based your salvation upon church attendance, church rituals, traditions and or good works, then it is misplaced.

While each of those are noble items, none of them will get you across the great gulf that separates us from God. Nothing we do can help us gain access to heaven and forgiveness for our sins. The gospel message is so powerful and wonderful because He crossed the gulf for us. He came to us as a babe in the manger 2,000 years ago. He lived a sinless life and sacrificed his life on a wooden cross. He paid the penalty we deserve for our sins. Our part is to simply trust and accept this gift of forgiveness.

Would you like to pray with me and put all doubts to rest? If you want to put your life in the hands of the Good Shepherd, cease striving to be good enough and simply lean on Jesus and His death for your sins, then pause here and pray,

"Dear God, I am *sorry* for my sins. *Thank you*, that you love me and that you died for me and my sins. *Please* come into my heart and life. I place my faith in you. Oh Lord, please make me the man or woman you desire me to be. Oh Lord, please give me your wisdom to pass on this eternal message to my children and grandchildren. In Jesus' name, AMEN."

If you just paused to pray this prayer to God for the first time and truly meant it from your heart, you are now my brother or sister in Christ! Praise God! Next, let me know of this decision by reaching out to me on my website at LoriJoinerMinistries.org. I can send you some free basic Bible studies to help you in your new walk with Christ.

The Bottom Line

Placing our faith in Christ and teaching our children and grandchildren how to do the same, is the most important step we can possibly take with our children now and for eternity. Don't put this important step off until tomorrow. Teach the gospel today, ask about salvation in Christ today and keep watch for opportunities to lead your children to personal faith in Christ.

Making the decision to place my faith in Christ is the best decision I have ever made, and I am thrilled my children have made this decision as well. I am already praying for the day when I can share the same message with my future grandchildren.

Chapter 5

Teach Your Children about the Great Commission

JESUS told his disciples, and now through scripture exhorts us to take the initiative to tell others about God and help them grow in Him. This teaching is known as the Great Commission, which is found in—

Mathew 28:18-20.

> [18]All authority in heaven and on earth has been given to me. [19] Therefore go and make disciples of all nations, baptizing them in the name of the Father and of the Son and of the Holy Spirit, [20] and teaching them to obey everything I have commanded you. And surely, I am with you always, to the very end of the age.

In this passage, we learn that sharing Christ with others and teaching them to obey Jesus' teachings is not an optional item in our lives. It is not something we do when we have time or just when we feel like it. He has already commissioned us, given us our marching orders, here in Matthew 28. It is now up to us to follow His direction.

As parents seeking to raise our children unto the Lord, we need to ensure our children understand this teaching as well. The Great Commission is not something our children do when they graduate from college, when they get a career or when they start a family. On the contrary, as soon as they understand the Great Commission, they can be involved in ministering to the lost.

In Luke 10:2, Jesus said, "The harvest is plentiful, but the workers are few. Ask the Lord of the harvest, therefore, to send out workers into his harvest field."

This verse illustrates that people who need to hear and receive Christ are all around us and plentiful. It is the responsibility of Christians to pray for laborers in the fields and be willing to serve as Christ-centered ambassadors while they reach out to the lost with the compassion and grace found in Jesus Christ.

Romans 10:13 says, "For everyone who calls on the name of the Lord will be saved."

We must boldly teach our children that people's eternal destinies can be changed because of Jesus. Our children, at a surprisingly young age, can be involved in the Great Commission and point people to Christ.

First, teach your children what the Great Commission is. Then, demonstrate how to fulfill the Great Commission.

Steps to help your children learn about and engage in the Great Commission:

1. Teach what the Bible has to say about this topic.

Choose a "Verse of the Week," and read it to your kids. Perhaps, write the verse on a small chalkboard in the kitchen where they grab their snacks or write it on the mirror in their bathrooms, so they can read the scriptures as they brush their teeth. Once a week at a meal, talk about that verse or any verse and explain the meaning. Choose verses that point to reaching others for Christ and helping others. Start with the verses I shared at the beginning of this chapter.

Alan reading the Bible to the boys.

2. Share the "why" behind the Great Commission.

Teach your children that as Christ-followers, one of the most awesome things we get to do is be a part of other people's lives as they go from unsaved to saved. Make it clear to your children that we are God's instruments and tools in His hands to share the gospel and help people trust Him. Let them know regularly what a thrill it is to be a person God can count on to share about His love, His forgiveness, and how He can turn our mess into our message! He can take the worst of sinners and save them and help them be a mighty instrument in God's kingdom.

3. Implement the "Caught than Taught" principle.

With my sons, even as I was formally teaching them about the Great Commission or even verses from the Bible that talked about this, I was already demonstrating it for them. This is the principle of "Caught than Taught". This emphasizes the principle that anything we want to teach our children will best be handed down if we demonstrate what we want to see happen, rather than merely teaching it. You can teach something all day long, but if your kids catch you actually doing what you taught them, this sticks in their minds and hearts better.

My children are seeing me engage in the Great Commission as they are growing up. For example, I recall one day at the pool visiting with a woman who was new to my area. As our children swam and bobbed around us, we simply chatted about any number of things. At one point, in front of my kids, I asked her if she was interested in finding a church to belong to and if she would like to come with me to mine. She said she would love to come. The following Sunday, she and her family met my family in the lobby of our church. We all walked the halls, checking each child into Sunday school classes and such. My children "caught" me asking spiritual questions about attending church at the pool that day. Next, they saw the follow through when we met them at church and helped them get settled. They "caught" what I did, and this enhanced what they were "taught."

My children have literally seen this scenario take place hundreds of times. Inviting people to church helps me find out where they are spiritually. Even if they say no, I am not offended. This is helpful information. I always respond by saying, "Ok, just know you are invited if you ever change your mind."

Let your children hear you ask spiritual questions or hear you invite others to church. Intentionally, do this in front of your children at the park, at swim lessons, at the end of a play date and chaperoning a field trip. Take steps of faith in front of your children. Let them hear you talk about Christ, church and Bible study. Allow them to hear you invite people to these activities and ask if you can pray for them. This is a powerful model and example to them.

My sons regularly invite their friends to church. They have heard me do it countless times, so for them, it is a natural way to do life. It's just what we do as believers and Christ-followers. We are fortunate to attend a church that offers numerous amazing activities and opportunities to invite guests.

My son, Josh, invites people to church all the time. One of my absolute favorite stories is when he was in third grade, and he invited his best friend to church. He came home from school one afternoon and told me he invited another child to church on the playground at school that day and asked if we could pick him up.

I texted the mom for permission, and she said it was ok for him to attend the following Sunday morning. She texted me that morning, I thought she was going to cancel, but instead she said, "I am so happy my son is joining you all for church. However, I am the one that really needs to go. Can my daughter and I join you as well?"

She not only came and even joined my church that day, but she also got plugged into a Bible study! She was eager to grow in Christ and be connected to a great church but had not started yet. My son's invitation to her son was the catalyst she needed.

That night, as I said Josh's prayers, I told him how proud of him I was. How his one invite had touched the lives of three people for Christ. I reiterated that this is what it means to be a part of the Great Commission–sharing God's love with people or at least bringing them to a place where they can hear and receive Jesus Christ as Lord and Savior.

This year, our church put on a youth event called Fall Riot. Josh invited his entire junior high lunch group to come to the church youth event. One child came who had never ever been to a church before. I again told Josh how proud of him I was that he invited others. We also prayed for the salvation of his friend.

My younger son, Jake, invited a friend to Vacation Bible School at our church. I picked this child up in my vehicle. One day as we walked in, I asked him if he understood what he was hearing and learning. He said he didn't really understand. He was from a home that did not attend any religious services. I asked him where he thought people went when they died, and he said, "I don't know, I guess the dump."

I was heartbroken he thought that! The great news is at VBS that very day he learned how each person can go to heaven when they die if they place their faith and trust in Christ, and he went for it! He raised his hand in the children's service and prayed to trust Christ as his Savior. Later, he was also baptized at our church. I told Jake how proud of him I was that he had invited this child to

Vacation Bible School and how God had used him to touch the life of another person for eternity.

Your kids are not too young to learn about the Great Commission. Start talking, demonstrating and reinforcing this vital biblical teaching. Your kids can lay up treasure in heaven starting now. Your kids can invite others to church and what they learn can change entire families for eternity!

I feel so passionate about teaching young children how to fulfill the Great Commission that I traded in my car a couple of years ago for a larger one for the very purpose of bringing kids to church. At the time, I owned a Mitsubishi Outlander. It was a great car that was paid-off and fit our family of four well, but there was just one problem. It could not fit anyone else comfortably. The back seat was very narrow and there was no third row. This broke my heart as my boys wanted to invite friends to church, but I could not fit more than one.

So, I talked with my husband about getting another car. He said, "Just so I understand, we have a car that is paid off, gives us absolutely no issues and fits our family perfectly, but you want another car?"

I said, "I need a van. I need to fit more kids in the car for church, Vacation Bible School and youth group meetings."

I had been taken to church by neighbors myself when I was in high school. A ride to church was how I was able to first hear the gospel message, and I absolutely wanted to pay that forward.

Soon we sold my Mitsubishi Outlander and purchased a used Dodge Caravan. Last week, my sons invited three of their friends to youth group, and we were elated to seat them all in our vehicle! When I drove the van to pick up the kids, we were thrilled.

Lori getting her minivan.

The Bottom Line

By engaging in the Great Commission, your kids can see their friends saved and transformed by Jesus Christ. Your children can be used by God and feel the delight of being a useful vessel in his hands!

Don't wait! Instead, ask them, "Who do you want to bring to church this week?"

That may be a tough question if they are not used to thinking of others who may need God, but simply brainstorm with them a person to invite.

How about you, mom and Dad? Who could you invite to church or Bible study this week and model this to your children?

Chapter 6

Make Christian Activities the Priority

OUR children are a gift from God. Not only should we be thankful for them, but we must also see their lives as a great stewardship. They are on loan to us from God. He has given them to us to raise unto Him, so God has to be absolutely first in their lives. As you know by now, I firmly believe we as parents are to take the reins when it comes to raising our children in the Lord. We need to think of their spiritual development and teach the basics of the Bible, salvation, morality and more.

Plugging into a great church and Christian programs and activities can be such a phenomenal source of reinforcement for your children's growing spiritual life.

I saw a great meme the other day that read, "Parents, one day our children will stand before King Jesus, and what will matter the most is not their grades, their popularity, their batting average, their class rank or their college transcripts. What will matter the most is their soul and what they did for Him throughout their lives."

God has entrusted my husband and me with our children's lives and spiritual development. We need to make certain He and His purposes on earth are talked about in the home and living for Him is modeled in the lives of each parent.

Joining Christian programs can be a great way to support your efforts to help your children build a solid foundation upon Christ.

I know many parents who are quick to put their children in sports, dance, piano, etc., but have done little to prioritize Christian activities. Again, many are simply leaving this to a Sunday morning, if that, routine at church, but I strongly suggest that as you look at your week, you layer in the things of the Lord first.

Three reasons to put God first in weekly activities:

1. **They will see other adults teaching children about God.**

When my sons attend church or youth group, they see that I am not the only one who is teaching the Bible and helping to build in them a strong foundation in Christ. Other adults can not only reiterate what I am teaching at home, but often may explain the same biblical content in a different way and thus help my children to grasp the concept better.

2. **They will make friends with other children who are learning about God.**

I have always prayed and asked the Lord to bring godly friends into my children's lives. Attending church activities is a great way to see this be a reality. I even go a step further and seek to set up play dates and hang outs with these families. I will approach the mom and say, "It seems our boys like hanging out together at church activities. Would you like to get them together during the week as well?" Just this past week a mom and her son came to my home and taught Josh and I a new board game. I am actively fostering Christian friendships for my children the best I can.

3. They will have help when facing temptation.

When children face temptations in life, the little league soccer practice will not help as much as the AWANA meeting. They are learning Bible verses, and God can bring scriptures to their mind the very moment they need them. When faced with compromising their beliefs and straying from what they know, the extra gymnastics lesson will not help as much as Wednesday night youth meeting, where they learn about standing firm for Christ.

Great Christian activities to consider for your child:

The local church

Find a church near you and join. Don't just attend but participate. Do the community service projects with your church, volunteer on your rotation in the nursery, teach in a Sunday school class, attend the retreats, attend youth group, bring the doughnuts or whatever is needed. Regular, local, in-person church attendance and participation is the best way to help your family and your children grow in Christ.

As a parent, you need to model what you hope will be true of your own children one day. Avoid watching church on the couch. No matter how awesome a certain preacher is, make the effort to attend a local church. The children in homes, where mom and dad are watching church from the couch are severely missing out on age-appropriate Bible lessons, fellowship and teaching. Children and youth need to be in a place where they can meet other Christian friends and need the support of each other in their faith in Christ during their junior high and high school years. This is tough to do from the couch. Local church attendance and involvement is key in making Christ and Christian activities a priority in your child's life.

Jake receiving an Awana award.

Awana

Awana is a world-wide nonprofit ministry focused on providing Bible-based evangelism and discipleship for ages 2-18. The name stands for "Approved Workmen Are Not Ashamed" from 2 Timothy 2:15. They are a global leader in child and youth discipleship. Awana gives children the opportunity to know, love and serve Jesus and is hosted in churches all over the globe. I registered my children for this program when they were young, and it is volunteer based. The children meet for 30 minutes of scripture memorization, 30 minutes of game time and 30 minutes of a Bible message for their age level. They earn awards for the verses they memorize.

Church youth group

Many churches offer a youth group, where kids generally from junior high to high school ages meet during the week for age-based Bible lessons, worship and fellowship. Check out your church's youth activities and options. You may even attend as a volunteer or visitor to check it out and encourage your children to do the same.

The biggest issue, however, is not if your church has a youth group, but making it a priority in your child's life. For example, my church has literally thousands of families involved on any given Sunday morning, but the youth group is not very large. Why? Priorities.

Many people do not prioritize the Lord in their weekly schedule. They tend to put many other activities before layering in godly activities. For my sons, Josh and Jake, church is *the* priority. Let me explain what this looks like and why this is the case in our home.

Josh is currently a year-round swimmer, and practice is every weeknight from 6:15 to 7:45. My husband and I pay monthly for lessons. Therefore, he will have the necessary skills, in the event, he ever wishes to try out for the high school team. But guess what night he does not go to practice? That would be Wednesday night because on Wednesday nights he goes to youth group. My husband said to me one day, "So we are paying for Josh to practice swimming with his team five nights a week.

However, he is only going four nights a week?" I responded, "Yes, you are correct. The extra laps he may get in on Wednesdays will not help him spiritually, and that is what matters in his life on earth and his life in eternity with God."

Josh and Lori enjoying a swim meet.

And as I stated in the last chapter, Josh does not simply attend youth group, he invites his friends from school to youth group, so they can hear the gospel message and perhaps trust Christ. Furthermore, he worships God with other kids his age and hears from great leaders teaching from the Bible. He is building friendships with other children in agreement with the same morals, values and biblical foundations he is being taught.

A few years ago, my younger son Jake was heavily involved in gymnastics. He had moved up through the levels of gymnastics at a great pace, and they offered him a spot on the gymnastics competitive team. We were thrilled to receive the official letter inviting him onto this special traveling competitive team. All that he had been working for had finally paid off.

However, when I asked about the program, my initial enthusiasm began to wane. First, I was shocked at the amount of money it would cost. I could have bought a new car based on the sticker price of being on a competitive travel gymnastics team. Secondly, the number of hours they wanted him to train daily at the gym surprised me. The practice time went from two hours per week to nine! Three days a week, I would be required to take him directly from school to gymnastics from 5 to 8 p.m. each night. I recognized that once he started, I wouldn't see my child very often. Then, when I learned practices took place on Monday, Wednesday and Friday nights, with no option to miss on Wednesday nights, this prevented him from being able to participate in Awana and youth group for the foreseeable future.

There were many other factors involved in our decision to turn down that coveted spot on the competitive gymnastics team, but I never had peace about him missing church on Wednesday nights. I thought, *Why would I take my child away from godly teaching, singing and Christian friendships to put him with a coach who may not be a Christian?* I thank God for the many talents He has given my sons, but I don't want those talents to distract from God being the priority in their lives.

Jake performing a handstand.

I share these two examples because I don't just preach this idea of making Christian activities a priority in your schedule. I am putting my money where my mouth is, and this is especially important during children's formative young years. The Lord comes first in our schedule, and I made tough decisions with this priority in mind.

I will give you this. Sports like gymnastics and swimming are individual sports, so if Josh does not attend swim practice on Wednesday nights, this will not hold other athletes back. Some of you reading this book may have children who are a part of a team sport, such as baseball and perhaps your child is the pitcher. It would be hard for that team to practice without the pitcher. Or your daughter may be a part of a cheer team, and she is the spotter. It would be challenging for that team to train without her doing her part. I do not want to be legalistic in this area. I do, however, want to encourage parents to think about this and make decisions with God in the equation.

Each season of life this must be thought through and analyzed. I have turned down, along with my children and my husband, possibly great opportunities because I know what will matter in life and in eternity is their relationships with the Lord, so I take this seriously. I fully recognize not every situation is as easy as mine have been up to this point.

Other great Christian organizations

Fellowship of Christian Athletes (FCA), Cru High (Campus Crusade for Christ) and Young Life are other organizations you can look into for your child. Search your school and area for great Christian organizations to point your children towards as they are learning and growing in their faith. The three I mentioned meet in junior high, high schools and colleges all over the nation.

Connect your child's talents to God

Connect your child's talents to the God who gave them that gift, skill, desire and joy. When Josh is about to compete in a swim meet, I pray for him out loud to do his best. I thank God for blessing him with a healthy body to be able to swim, with the perseverance to practice each day (for miles upon miles sometimes) and that he has something in his life he enjoys so much.

Whether it is ballet, piano, wrestling, art, computer programming, skateboarding, skiing or gymnastics, whatever the interest is, God gave it to them. He blessed them with the mind, the body, the opportunity, the will and the desire. As parents, we should point them to God in their activities. Remind them that God gave them those talents, and He has a great plan for them to use this for His glory.

The Bottom Line

Moms and dads, make Christian activities a priority in your own life and in the lives of your children as they're growing. Model this for them. Talk out loud as to what you do in your schedule to prioritize God each week. Remind them how there are only four things which will last for eternity: God, His Word, His Kingdom and the souls of mankind. These are the items to be layered in and prioritized in our lives and the lives of our children.

Chapter 7

Read Christian Books to Your Children

AS parents, we must understand just how important it is to read out loud to our children, especially when they are young. This practice will greatly enhance your efforts to raise your children unto the Lord. While our children are growing, we need to be mindful not to let go of this practice too soon. Furthermore, it is never too early or too late to start reading out loud to your children. If this is not happening, especially if your kids are in elementary, start now.

Learning to read is a process beginning long before a child starts school. The American Academy of Pediatrics recommends parents start reading to their children from birth. When parents or grandparents read out loud to their children, even when they are infants, they are helping build important foundational literacy skills. Children over time learn that text and those scribbles on the page have meaning. Each time you read, the child picks up and develops new vocabulary, and over time, they embrace reading as not only enjoyable but a way of life. There is a saying that states, "Readers are leaders."

When Josh and Jake were little, I read to them a great deal. I was always reading at naptime, bedtime, quiet time and as much as I could fit into each day. We went to the local library every 2 to 3 weeks and would go home with bags of books to have new things to read each night.

Reading helps a child's Christian and academic development. This chapter focuses on why you should read to your children and then will transition to the many books I read to my own children.

Three reasons to read to your children often:

1. **Reading to your children will help their cognitive development.**

Cognitive development affects how children think, learn and how they explore. Reading helps stimulate this function in their brain, helps them to acquire and process information, and appropriate the correct response to information. By reading to your children, they will literally learn more words and the meanings. I always loved pointing out words that could have two meanings. I would say, "Does this word mean a bear 'Rarrrrr', or the shelf is bare? Does this word mean a pen I write with, or a pin I use when sewing?" My boys are now in high school and junior high, and I still do this. I am always looking to sharpen their vocabulary and word skills.

2. **Reading to your children is good for their memory.**

When you read your child a story, ask them a question about it when you are finished. They will be tested on this later in school. It's called comprehension. Are they able to recall what you read to them? You may read a story about a child who is scared of the dark. Ask your child about that scenario. Can they remember a detail? Can they recall why the child was scared? Can they relate it to their own lives?

Of course, my kids had their favorite books they wanted me to read so often they could eventually recite the entire story from memory. My sons can quote *One Hungry Monster* from start to finish to this day because they loved it so much!

3. **Reading to your children is good for their Christian spiritual development.**

Out of all the great reasons to read to your children, the number one reason is to read to them about the Christian faith. When I would go to the library, I do not recall finding a lot of Christian books for children. Maybe there were some, but those I had to purchase. I could find *Cloudy with a Chance of Meatballs* by Judi Barrett, *Biscuit Goes to School* by David Shannon, books by Shel Silverstein, Dr. Seuss and other literary materials. But when it came to books about God, I had to search for them and purchase them. I filled my children's shelves with Christian literature from an early age.

I first read my boys *A is for Adam,* which is a large hardback book with bright colors and big pictures. In this book, each letter of the alphabet introduces a basic Christian teaching. We read this book countless times. Another I read to my sons was *My Creation Bible,* which is a children's book about creation, mankind, animals, Jesus and other topics. I bought both of these books from the ministry Answers in Genesis (answersingenesis.org). This ministry site is a phenomenal place to find Christ-centered books for children of all ages.

As my boys were learning to read in their preschool years, I was able to purchase several *I Can Read* books of basic Bible stories from ZonderKidz. Each book contained one short Bible story. As they were learning to read, they could eventually identify some of the words. It was so thrilling to hear them begin to read basic Bible stories themselves.

As my sons entered elementary, I bought them the *Answers Book for Kids: 20 Questions from Kids.* Each small hardback book covers topics such as —

- Creation & the Fall
- Dinosaurs & the Flood of Noah
- Sin, Salvation and the Christian Life
- God & the Bible
- Space & Astronomy
- Babel & the Ice Age
- Satan & Angels

My kids are older now, and at bedtime, they are reading chapter books on their own. They do so much reading that now I have to go into their rooms an hour after bedtime to make them put the books down and go to sleep.

I still want to read together, so I can answer their questions or explain something to them. This past summer, each afternoon during lunch, I read to them from a book called *Talking with Your Kids about God: 30 Conversations Every Christian Parent Must Have* by Natasha Crain. This is no lightweight book. It is an in-depth book about weighty spiritual topics such as the existence of God, science and God, the nature of God and believing in God.

Each day we read together and discuss. They do not argue with me when I mention we will be reading during lunch. Reading is just part of the culture of our home.

Lori reading to the boys on long road trips.

They did not say, "I want to watch cartoons, or I want to watch a video." Again, I started the reading as a part of my parenting long ago. So, in a way, reading around the table or on the couch or at night is just normal.

One summer we took a road trip to see our extended family in Kentucky. On that trip, I read to them the book called *The Case for Christ for Kids* by Lee Strobel. This is a great resource to answer the questions that kids aged 8-12 often ask about Jesus such as —

- Historical evidence, and scientific proof backing up what the Bible says
- Kid-friendly stories that make the facts easy to understand
- Ways to talk to other people about Jesus
- The book also includes illustrations and graphics to make the topics memorable.

I did not want them to zone out while I read to them the important information in this book, so I decided I would quiz them after every chapter. For each right answer, they would earn one dollar. I would read a chapter, then create questions from the chapter to quiz them with. They each earned a ton of money by the time we reached Kentucky, but even more, they really listened to the helpful spiritual information.

Buy Christian books year-round

I often purchase Christian books as gifts for my children. At Easter, Christmas, and birthdays, they are gifted with age-appropriate Christian books. Not just Lego sets, not just Nerf guns, not just clothes, but books, and Christian books at that. This past Christmas, I bought my son, Josh, the book *My Name Is Tani and I Believe in Miracles: The Amazing True Story of One Boy's Journey from Refugee to Chess Champion.* I picked this book up at Mardel, a local Christian bookstore in my city. I also bought Jake, my other son, some graphic novels about Bible stories.

At Easter, stick a Christian book in their basket. At Christmas, place an age-appropriate book under the tree. On their birthday, surprise them with a new Christian daily devotional. Books, devotionals, Bibles and scripture bookmarks are all helpful in pointing your children to

God in each phase and stage of your child's life. When school was out this past Spring, I had a new Christian book for them to read this summer waiting on their beds. This time I chose books about men and women who were standing for Christ in their lives in unique ways.

The Bottom Line

Don't put off reading to your kids and filling their shelves and minds with great Christian resources. Go to AnswersinGenesis.org at each milestone and order books which will help your child now and for eternity. Go to Mardel Christian bookstore or any of your local Christian bookstores and purchase age-appropriate Christian books and read them with your child. Give books on birthdays and holidays to family and relatives. And if you have not already done so, create a culture in your home of reading. This culture will serve you so well as your children age, and you can keep giving them faith-based books. Even when my boys are in high school and college, I will be searching for faith-based, Christ-centered books to give them to enrich and strengthen their faith.

Chapter 8

Teach Your Children an Eternal Perspective

AN eternal perspective is idea of focusing not just on the here and now, but also about life *after* this life. The life where we will live eternally with Christ if we have placed our faith in Jesus. If we only think about this life, we will neglect to prepare for the longer, eternal life with Him.

As we raise our children unto the Lord, it is paramount that we teach them not to simply live for now, but also for eternity. This can be a challenging concept for them to grasp. However, as parents, we can begin to lay the groundwork for this perspective when our children are young and then build upon this at each age and stage of their life.

Having an eternal perspective helps me personally a great deal. It reminds me to keep the main things the main things in my life and not get too caught up in things which won't matter all that much in light of eternity. Thinking about Heaven helps me persevere here on earth, helps me grieve, helps me endure hardship and helps me survive really challenging situations. Knowing my time on earth is finite is one of the cornerstones of my faith. So, I have absolutely taught this to my sons, and I want to encourage you to teach it to your children as well.

Consider what the Bible has to teach us about this important topic—

James 4:14 "Why, you do not even know what will happen tomorrow. What is your life? You are a mist that appears for a little while and then vanishes."

Psalm 144:4 "Man is like the breath; His days are like a passing shadow."

1 Corinthians 3:10-15 "[10] By the grace God has given me, I laid a foundation as a wise builder, and someone else is building on it. But each one should build with care. [11] For no one can lay any foundation other than the one already laid, which is Jesus Christ. [12] If anyone builds on this foundation using gold, silver, costly stones, wood, hay or straw, [13] their work will be shown for what it is, because the Day will bring it to light. It will be revealed with fire, and the fire will test the quality of each person's work. [14] If what has been built survives, the builder will receive a reward. [15] If it is burned up, the builder will suffer loss but yet will be saved–even though only as one escaping through the flames."

Examining 1 Corinthians 3:10-15 a little deeper

Verses 10-11 teach that Christ himself is the foundation for the church. When Paul said he laid the foundation of the church in Corinth, he meant by founding it. When he went there and preached about Christ, how He was crucified and was raised from the dead, people began to put their faith in Christ. The church in Corinth was founded and began to grow. Christ is the foundation of the church, and He is also our foundation personally.

Verses 12-13 teach that our works will be examined. Gold, silver and costly stones refer to or are symbols of items which lead to pleasing Christ and building His church and His kingdom on earth. Things such as sound doctrine, pure motives, serving others, sharing the gospel message and teaching scripture correctly, unlike cults who teach an adulterated version of scripture. All these are items which please God.

Wood, hay and straw are items which won't last for eternity. These items include but are not limited to proclaiming a religion based on good works or being a good person, using time and money only for temporal purposes and living a selfish, self-centered life, not a Christ-centered life. These are items which displease God and do not result in treasure in heaven.

In verse 13, "The Day" refers to the day when the believer will stand before God and give an account of the stewardship of his or her life at Christ's Judgment Seat. Many Christians have not heard or not taken seriously, the Judgment Day of Christ. Sadly, they are unaware of the upcoming judgment of their works with fire.

Understand that the Judgment Seat of Christ is only for believers in Jesus. Only for those who have Christ as their foundation. The purpose of the

Judgment Seat is not to punish sin, as our sin has already been dealt with at the cross. Instead, God is looking for things to reward!

2 Corinthians 5:10, "For we must all appear before the Judgment Seat of Christ, that each one may receive what is due him for the things done while in the body, whether good or bad."

Verse 13 explains how our works will be revealed with fire. Fire is used throughout scripture as a purifying agent or a consuming force. When I picture my works being tested with fire, I picture all of my wood, hay and straw piled with my gold, silver costly stones and being lit on fire. The fire, in one instant, will purify and consume all which was not eternal. Some believers will be left with nothing. They will still be with Christ but will have nothing of praise to present to Christ, nothing for Christ to reward.

These verses in scripture remind me of my husband burning brush piles. It takes him months and months of work to push huge amounts of old dead trees, bushes, roots and limbs all into a huge heap. Then, in just mere hours, it is all burned up! Nothing but ashes is left. Just a black smudge on the ground. Magnify that by a million-fold and you get a sense of what is awaiting many Christians at the Judgment Seat of Christ. So much of what we do is going to burn up.

One thing I want you to understand is that we all have wood, hay and straw. Our motives for doing things are not always pure; we do not always make right Christ centered decisions. We do not always yield to the Holy Spirit.

Verses 14-15 teach about reward. How God will reward us is incomprehensible to our finite limited minds. However, the rewards are worth it or else why would God have so strongly urged us to prepare for them? We can be sure God's rewards should be looked forward to. They are the healthy motivation we need to persevere under trial.

1 Corinthians 2:9 "No eye has seen, no ear has heard, no mind has conceived what God has prepared for those who love him."

Verse 15 says some people will escape through flames. We read there will be some plucked from the fire. The person themself will be saved but will have nothing to show for their life. Nothing for Christ to reward.

If you have never learned or studied about the Judgment Seat of Christ, I would highly recommend the book *This Was Your Life: Preparing to Meet God Face to Face* by Rick Howard and Jamie Lash. This was a pivotal book in my formative years as a young Christ follower, I have read it over ten times, and I use this book with the women I disciple to this day.

In light of this biblical teaching, we can see how very important it is to teach our children about heaven, the Judgment Seat of Christ, and laying up treasure in heaven. Don't merely teach them to read, add and subtract. Don't merely teach them to mow the lawn, buy a house and get a good job. Teach them an eternal, godly, biblically sound perspective. The perspective that we are not here long, but what we do here on earth really matters in eternity.

Tips to teach your children to have an eternal perspective:

1. **Teach your children eternal perspective Bible verses.**

   With my sons, I may at breakfast or at lunch ask, "Boys, did you know the Bible says our life is like a mist which appears for a while then vanishes? What do you think that means?" Depending on the age level of your kids, you will get varying answers, but the point is you need to at least read these verses to them. Feel free to use any of the verses I chose at the beginning of this chapter to get you started.

2. **Use a hand motion or sound to reinforce eternal perspective.**

   I will sometimes snap my fingers and say, "Boys, this is all we've got. When you think about our 100 years on earth in comparison to eternity, it's like a snap," and I snap my fingers. It may feel long now, but we will look back on this time from eternity and say, "Wow… that went by fast." I will explain that what we do with our "snap" matters and how life is a gift, a short gift, to be lived for God.

3. **Teach eternal perspective through prayer.**

When praying for my sons out loud in the mornings I will say, "Oh Lord, thank you that Josh is awake for another day on earth, another day to serve you, and another day to lay up treasure in heaven and to please you. Thank you, Lord, that earth is not his final destination. He is here to learn and grow and develop into the man you desire him to be. Thank you, he has a place in heaven already, a heavenly citizenship. He is just passing through."

4. **Use the bank account analogy when teaching to have an eternal perspective.**

I have taught my sons on numerous occasions how no one knows how many days are in their bank account of life. For this reason, we need to be good stewards of each day as only God knows the number of days we have on earth. I turned 50 years old this past week and told them I am thankful for each day I have had. I added that however many more days the Lord grants me, I will continue to dedicate to raising them up to be godly leaders for their generation to share the love of God and salvation in Christ.

5. **Explain how each person has one shot to live for eternity.**

I tell my sons that they have one shot. "Boys, listen up. We have one shot," I will say. "We have one shot to live life and then to stand before God and give an account of our lives. And God wants to say, 'Well done thy good and faithful servant.'" He wants to say this. Why else would he have given us so many verses and teachings on this subject throughout scripture? He is getting us ready and prepared, but we must heed his instructions.

Jesus told his disciples and others listening to his teaching in Mathew 6:19-20, "Do not lay up treasure on earth where moth and rust destroy and thieves break in and steal but lay up treasure in heaven where moth and rust do not destroy, and thieves do not break in and steal."

Boys learned to have an eternal perspective at church.

We really have such a brief time to lay up treasure in heaven, to persevere through trials, to get trained up to share our faith, disciple others, to invite people to church. We only get one shot to help fulfill the Great Commission. Mom and Dad, we get one shot.

- One shot to raise up the next godly generation
- One shot to further the Great Commission in our lifetime
- One shot to kick the ball down the Great Commission field
- One shot to shine the light of Christ here on earth

This breath, this life, this vapor can be squandered away on selfish living, temporal mindset, small petty issues or can be used to bring glory to God and add to His eternal kingdom. We need to explain to our children that life is a gift. Your children should not see life as a chore to get through. Please do not let that be your mantra about life. Be thankful. Let them hear you pray, "Thank you Lord, we have another day with you! Another day to learn about you, grow in our love for you and be used by you to help others. Another day to lay up treasure in heaven."

Be incredibly intentional about teaching your children to view life through an eternal perspective. Teach an eternal perspective to your children all through their ages and stages, always pointing to the fact that life is a gift from God, our citizenship is in heaven, and that we have one shot to make this life count for Him.

A Balanced Perspective

I have emphasized extensively in this chapter about living for eternity, laying up treasure in heaven and not simply living for what we can get and do now. However, there is a balance to this topic. Having a relationship with Christ and walking with Him has absolutely helped in the here and now as well.

I share with my sons often about the countless times God has helped me now, on earth. Any time I am reminded of a past answered prayer, I love to share it with my sons, so they know how walking with God can benefit them now on earth, not just in eternity. One of my favorite answered prayers took place my junior year of college at the University of North Texas.

When I attended college, I was barely making it financially. Thankfully, my junior year I received an academic scholarship, but it was not enough to pay my room and board. I worked a part time job. However, the pay did not cover even a fraction of my school expenses. That year, things got even worse as my parents filed bankruptcy, and they could not help me at all financially. My father told me on the phone I may need to return home, pause college and work or at least, return home and go to college somewhere else. I was distraught. I prayed for God to help me.

I then decided to apply for a Resident Assistant (RA) position. If I secured this job, I would be in charge of a dorm floor of students working for the housing department of the university. This job would cover my room and board, which included a single room with an extra $100 pay per month for living expenses. This seemed like a dream come true, until I got some disturbing news.

My heart sank when I learned 60 other people applied for the same job, and there were only 6 openings. I prayed and asked God to help me land one of those 6 open positions. The interview process began, and there were three rounds. Each round I made it through I praised God. I needed this job. My education depended on it.

One of the rounds they put us in scenarios and asked tough questions. By God's grace my suitemate at the time had been an RA at another college and helped me prepare how to answer the questions. We role played together as she corrected and helped me. What a gift God put in my path before I even knew I would need her assistance!

The final round came when we were interviewed by different residence hall directors. I had 5 interviews. I went to class each morning, rushed back to my room and got all dressed up, walked again across campus for an interview where I was asked more tough questions. In each interview, I navigated standing strong in my conviction as a Christ follower, but also showing I could handle a variety of situations with people who may not believe as I did. Each interview I thanked God for the opportunity. I also began to pray for a particular dorm to hire me. I would have taken any RA job in any residence hall, but I asked God specifically for a certain dorm, Kerr Hall. I liked the layout, the cafeteria on their first floor, the location on campus, and the people I had met there throughout the interview process.

After all the interviews were over, and I had made it through all three rounds we were told that if we got a phone call, we would be hired. If we did not get a phone call, then we could reapply the next semester for an RA job. I prayed for a phone call. This was before cell phones! I felt glued to my phone in my dorm room. I waited and waited and waited. I remember getting on my knees and asking God for this job. The fear of having to go home, the fear of not finishing college at this university and the fear of money problems in general haunted me, but I kept giving it to God in prayer. Then, I got a phone call.

The director of Kerr Hall called offering me and RA job. I was stunned, speechless and promptly accepted. She gave me a few details, but I could not even remember them. Joy unthinkable welled up in my heart and was about to burst forth! As I hung up the phone, the tears began to flow, tears of relief that I now had the money to stay in college. Tears of gratefulness to God for guiding me through the process and answering my heartfelt prayers.

As 60 students tried to land one of 6 positions, God's hand of blessing was upon me. He provided not just a job, but a job in Kerr Hall as I wanted. He has done this OVER and OVER. He answers my prayers fully and abundantly.

I teach my sons that yes, we will spend eternity with God, and we need to prepare for that destination diligently while on earth. I also teach them walking with God benefits us now.

God has gifted me with new cars, incredible places to live, money to buy nice things. He has helped me publish books, start a non-profit and kept me safe. Recall the ways God has blessed you now, answered your prayers now and in the past and share those with your children. Teach them how walking with God throughout life on earth has immense benefits and blessings for now and eternity.

The Bottom Line

The world's system naturally teaches that this is all there is. To live for self, find the easy way and store up treasures on earth. The Bible teaches another perspective. An eternal perspective keeps an eye on Heaven as we sojourn through life on this planet. We need to have this perspective as parents, and it must overflow into our actions, attitudes and relationships with others. Most importantly, we need to teach this biblical perspective to our children. And the best part,

God is here with us now, helping us now, answering our prayers, and preparing us for an eternity with Him!

Chapter 9

Point Your Children to Christ on Special Days of the Year

HOLIDAYS and birthdays are joyous times of gifts, family and time spent together. However, if you are not careful, toys, money and business can crowd out the opportunity to keep Christ in the picture during these special yearly milestones. As you raise your children unto the Lord, keep Him first place throughout the year by being intentional when it comes to holidays and birthdays.

Here are some helpful tips for you to use during these important holidays during the year to reinforce Christian teachings and continue to invest in your child's growing faith with God.

Christmas

Each Christmas, I do a few things which are now traditions in our family. Each is now on autopilot and is an opportunity place to point my children to Christ each Christmas season. Some of these ideas you may already be doing with your kids, and others you may consider implementing this year.

1. Bake a Happy Birthday, Jesus Cake.

Each Christmas we make a cake and decorate it for Jesus' birthday. I take a picture of my boys with this cake, and we even sing Happy Birthday to Jesus. I have done this since the boys were little and have continued even now that they are in junior high and high school. My sons knew early on that Christmas was about Jesus's birth, not Santa Claus, not Elf on the Shelf, but Jesus and Him being born. They understand Jesus is the best Christmas gift the world has ever known and a yummy cake which all can enjoy is a tasty way to reinforce this biblical teaching.

Josh and Jake holding the Happy Birthday Jesus cake.

2. Use Advent Boxes to keep the focus on Christ.

Many years ago, I was wandering through a Hallmark store when I saw these adorable tiny wooden boxes, all stacked up like a pyramid, each with its own little door painted in Christmas colors. It was so cute I had to buy it, and of course, I then had to purchase two as I could foresee my two sons fighting over who got to open the little door each day!

The first year of using the advent boxes, I simply put a little chocolate in each door, or a few coins or a dollar bill folded up. They loved opening the boxes and seeing the tiny surprise. We did this each day of December, but the next year, I wanted the focus to be on Christ.

Since then, when the boys open a box, there is a piece of paper inside. The paper inside has something written to point them to Christ. For example, one year each piece of paper had one verse from the book of Luke teaching about the events leading up to the birth of Christ. Another year, each paper had a name of God from the Bible such as Wonderful Counselor, Mighty Savior and Jehovah Jireh along with the corresponding verse to go with it.

This year, I did a verse about who they are because of Christ, which read, "I am loved. I am forgiven. I am saved, and I am a citizen in Heaven." Each day the boys opened the boxes, read the statement along with the verse, and we talked about how if not for the life of Christ, His birth, death and resurrection, we would be lost, unsaved and unforgiven.

Now, year after year, I run off and cut out little verses of one theme or another and stuff them in the boxes for them to read. I love the idea that each day of December they are learning something about God, and I am reinforcing the season is about Christ.

Now don't think I took the fun out of it, though! I still give them little gifts each day. Some of the gifts include money, like dollar bills or coins, some days it is candy and chocolate, and other days they get my highly valued coupons. These are coupons for a free dessert, extra iPad time, a no chores day and more.

These boxes serve to keep the focus on Jesus during the Christmas season.

Understand you don't have to have the little boxes I have to make this work. Many of you reading this are crafty and can probably come up with an even better idea than I have. It could be so simple such as a set of 25 envelopes that they open each day with scripture inside and a note that says, "Let's play bingo," or "You have a treat hidden in the Christmas tree," or "Let's make cookies today!" So have fun with it! Setting your child's heart toward Christ in a fun way all through December is the goal.

3. **Read the book of Luke in December.**

The book of Luke in the Bible is 24 chapters long, so one year we read as a family a chapter of the book of Luke after dinner each evening. To help the boys pay attention, I quizzed them after each chapter, and they earned cold hard cash if they could answer my questions. My husband came up with the questions, and sometimes I answered them accidentally. Alan would look at me like, "Lori, this is for the kids!"

I absolutely loved that they woke up on Christmas morning having read the entire book of Luke. That year, at ages 9 and 11, they fully understood why we were celebrating Christmas.

4. **Have something Christ-related under the tree.**

Amidst all the gifts you may give your children, have something that is Christ-related and age-appropriate. It could be a few books you picked up at a Christian bookstore, Christian coloring books if they are young, a Christian t-shirt, poster, bookmark, new Bible, new Bible cover, necklace, bracelet, framed picture or verse.

Easter

When it comes to celebrating Easter, I am doing a few similar things I do with Christmas. For example, in their Easter basket, I include something Christ-centered. We attend the Easter Service at our church, and my church even offers a Passion Week experience for children and adults. This is where you learn about all the events leading up to Jesus' death, burial and resurrection. I have no problem with egg hunts and baskets, but Easter is about the fact that Jesus died for our sins. He was buried in a tomb and was raised to life three days later. That story is read in our home, at church, and we celebrate with Christ centered baskets and such. Children should know, from an early age, what Easter really is about, not just the commercialism from the world's perspective.

Birthdays

The tradition in the Joiner home is that on their birthdays, to mark their new year, my sons wake up to about 30 signs all over the house that say things like, "Only a 14-year-old can sit here," or "This is a 14-year-old's lunch box," or "Only a 14-year-old can drink from this cup." Just silly signs everywhere marking their new year, but in the midst of those signs are verses like-Psalm 139:14, which says, "You are wonderfully made." Or I will make a sign that reads, "I am so glad God created YOU!"

Be intentional

This year, as you plan holiday events and birthday parties, pray and ask God to give you creative ideas for your family. You are free to use any of my ideas, but I trust God will give you ideas as well to help you to use holidays and birthdays to point your children to Christ.

The Bottom Line

Keeping the fun in holidays while also using them to reinforce Christian teachings is such a great and simple way to remember to layer in the Lord in your household celebrations. By being intentional, you can have Christ-centered celebrations that point your kids to Christ. When your children are opening gifts and being delighted at new toys and gadgets, you will feel a peace in your heart knowing you took the extra time to also fill their hearts and minds with a biblical teaching and encouragement.

Chapter 10

Teach Your Children about Baptism

BAPTISM is the first step of obedience after a person places their faith in Christ. It is a beautiful and powerful symbol of what God has done in saving us. As you raise your children unto the Lord, baptism needs to be talked about and explained clearly and early in their lives.

In chapter 3, I shared at length about sharing the gospel message with your children. You may recall that the gospel message, also called the "Good News" is the biblical teaching of salvation and it includes these four truths:

1. God loves us.
2. We are sinful.
3. Jesus Christ died on the cross to pay the penalty of our sins.
4. We must individually trust Christ as Savior and Lord.

And when our children come to the point where they place their faith in Christ, the next step for them is to be baptized. Explaining to your children what baptism is, from an early age, will be helpful for when in the future they take this step of obedience for themselves.

Jesus taught about baptism.

In Matthew 28:19-20, recall Jesus said, "Go and make disciples of all nations, baptizing them in the name of the

Father and of the Son and of the Holy Spirit, teaching them to obey everything I have commanded you. And surely, I am with you always, to the very end of the age."

We can deduct from these verses that the church, and the believers in the church, are responsible to—

- Teach Jesus' word.
- Make disciples.
- Baptize those disciples.
- This was to be done everywhere,
- And until the end of time.

Since Jesus commanded baptism it is important for us to heed what He said and obey.

Baptism is an outward symbol of an inward decision.

The inward decision comes first.

When a person places their faith in Christ, that is an inward decision. They have chosen to ask God to forgive their sins and give them the gift of eternal life with Him. At that moment, this person has been saved from hell. Salvation is a free gift of God and is not based on good works.

Ephesians 2:8-9 states, "[8] For it is by grace you have been saved, through faith—and this is not from yourselves, it is the gift of God [9] not by works, so that no one can boast."

The outward symbol, baptism, is next.

Baptism is a public profession of that inward decision. It's the opportunity for a person to put their "flag" up for Christ, so to speak and publicly identify with Christ. Water baptism is a beautiful picture of what our Lord has done for us. Complete immersion symbolizes our burial with our Lord; we are symbolically baptized into His death on the cross and are no longer slaves to self or sin. When we are raised out of the water, we are symbolically resurrected — raised to new life in Christ to be with Him forever.

Baptism is important, and it is an act of obedience we should carry out if for no other reason than to simply follow Christ's example. He himself was baptized in the Jordan River by John the Baptist. This is mentioned in all four gospel accounts. You can start in Matthew 3:13 or Mark 1:9 to get started if you would like to read it for yourself.

There are many more verses in the Bible as well as many books written on this topic. As a side note, if you would like to dive into this topic more, just go to GotQuestions.org and type in the word "baptism" and you will get a list of great, biblically based articles on this subject.

Tips to teach children about baptism:

1. **Take your children to see a person be baptized.**

The next time your church has a person baptized, go to the baptism. Let your child see this take place. My church has an outside baptismal and after church, each week, people who have placed their faith in Christ can go outside and be baptized. My children and I have seen people be baptized numerous times. When they were little, I explained what it meant. That this person has placed their faith in Christ, and they were letting their friends, family and other people in attendance know they are on God's side now.

2. **Read to them verses about baptism from the Bible.**

Read to them the verses found in Matthew 28:19-20, which I included at the beginning of this chapter. Then, explain what the word "baptize" means. It means letting others know you are now a Christ follower. We do this by going underwater and coming back up. You can also read to them about Jesus being baptized in Matthew 3:13 and Mark 1:9.

The children's ministry at my church took each Sunday School class of kids to the baptismal one Sunday morning and showed them everything about it. The children got to see where people change their clothes, the faucet which turns on the water and the tub-like structure holding all the water. Next, a lesson was given about what baptism is, which is publicly proclaiming you have placed your faith in Christ.

3. **Explain your own baptism story to your children.**

Do your children know your story? Teach it to them. My sons know that when I was 16, I got on my knees and placed my faith in Christ. They know a week or so later, I went back to church on a Sunday evening and was baptized. I shared the details of how I was asked publicly if Jesus was my Lord and Savior, and I said, "Yes". I told them how I held my breath when I went under the water and how the church gave me a change of clothes to wear, so I could change back into my dry clothes when I was finished.

When we explain to our children step by step what it is, where it happens and why people do it, this encourages them not to be afraid. It normalizes baptism and sets them up well for their baptism in the future.

***NOTE:* Baptism is not salvation or a prerequisite for salvation.**

Before I share the story of my children being baptized and how we celebrated that important milestone, I want to make one point extremely clear. Baptism is not, I repeat, *not* salvation or a prerequisite for salvation. You do not have to be baptized to be saved. Baptism does not save you. It is only an outward symbol of an inward decision to follow Christ and place your trust in Him.

When I explain this to my sons and to the women I disciple, I turn to the account of the thief on the cross in Luke 23:39–43, which says,

> 39 One of the criminals who hung there, hurled insults at him: 'Aren't you the Messiah? Save yourself and us!'
> 40 But the other criminal rebuked him. 'Don't you fear God,' he said, 'since you are under the
> same sentence? 41 We are punished justly, for we are getting what our deeds deserve. But this man has done nothing wrong.'
> 42 Then he said, 'Jesus, remember me when you come into your kingdom.'
> 43 Jesus answered him, 'Truly I tell you, today, you will be with me in paradise.'

Just observe from this passage how this thief on the cross, this self-confessed sinner, had no opportunity to hop down off his cross and get water baptized. However, he confessed faith in Jesus and Jesus replied, "Today, you will be with me in paradise."

Never scare a child or an adult for that matter into thinking they are not saved if they have not been baptized. We want them to be baptized as a step of obedience to Jesus' command in Matthew 28, but please don't dangle salvation over them or anyone else because of baptism status.

Both my sons placed their faith in Christ early in life. One I led to Christ at his bedside on Easter when he was 5. The other trusted Christ at church during a children's event, but both had apprehensions about baptism.

Even though I had taught them clearly what it was about, and they were involved in a great children's ministry, where they learned about baptism on their level. They still did not want to be baptized. I talked with my husband about this, and he asked me to let it go and let them make the decision when they were ready. He asked me not to push them but to trust God and let them decide.

I prayed over the years that God would bring them to the place where they would follow the Lord in believers' baptism. Every once in a while, I said to one of them, "Sweetheart, just so you know if you ever want to walk forward and be baptized, I will go with you." Or "You let me know when you are ready, and I will set it up at church." However, over the years they just resisted. I could not understand why, but I entrusted them to the Lord.

Then in October of 2021, both were in a youth meeting on a Wednesday night. The youth pastor asked if anyone wanted to be baptized, and both boys went forward. You can imagine my shock when they told me on the way home that they were getting baptized soon! I was like what?!

I am so glad I trusted the Lord and let them make the decision. I wanted them to be baptized on their own and not out of fear or me persuading them. This needed to be between them and the Lord.

Josh and Jake are all smiles after baptism.

We arranged the baptism to be a few weeks later, and you had better believe I made a big deal out of it! I had my family come in town, and we had lunch afterward at my home. Both boys had gifts to open such as new Bibles and Bible covers. On the inside of their Bibles, I wrote their names and the date they got baptized. We prayed over them as a family to be mighty men in God's Kingdom and to shine a light for Christ wherever God may lead them. I told them how proud of them I was for *Putting Their Flag Up for Christ.*

The Bottom Line

Raising our children unto the Lord includes being clear about how to trust Christ as Savior and how to be baptized. When your child, or disciple for that matter, places his or her faith in Christ and is baptized, take pictures, go to lunch, buy gifts and celebrate this step of obedience and the decision to publicly confess that Jesus Christ is their Lord! If you have not personally been baptized yet, don't put this off. It is an important step of obedience unto the Lord. It will also serve as a powerful witness for your family and children to observe.

Chapter 11

Teach Your Children to Embrace Being Different

As parents, we need to be at peace with our lives and our children's lives being different from others. We need to embrace, as a fact, that we are indeed different. Our Christian families should look and act differently than our neighbors, our co-workers and the world in general. You need to own this and not try to conform to the customs, habits and patterns of others.

We are set apart as God's chosen people. We will not watch the same movies other families watch, make the same decisions, frequent the same restaurants, dress the same, spend our money the same or use our time the same as others. Don't be embarrassed by this; it is simply a fact. As we raise our children unto the Lord, we need to make it clear we are not ashamed of being different. On the contrary, we are blessed because of our dedication to Christ.

Read here what God told Moses to say to the Israelite people about this very fact.

Leviticus 18:1-5 "Then the Lord said to Moses, '2 Give the following instructions to the people of Israel. I am the Lord, your God. 3 So do not act like the people in Egypt, where you used to live, or like the people of Canaan, where I am taking you. You must not imitate their way of life. 4 You must obey all my regulations and be careful to obey my decrees, for I am the Lord your God.

5 If you obey my decrees and my regulations, you will find life through them. I am the Lord.'"

Leviticus 20:26 "You must be holy because I, the Lord, am holy. I have set you apart from all other people to be my very own."

When a person places their faith in Christ, they are a new creation. The Holy Spirit comes to reside in their life, begins to bear fruit of the Spirit and helps the person cease bearing the fruit of the flesh as is outlined in Galatians chapter 5. According to 1 Corinthians chapter 3, when we become Christians, we will begin to act differently because we are different. We are born again, spiritually new, with the Holy Spirit, who is God, now residing in and directing our lives.

These verses illustrate that as God's people, we are different because we follow God, and we are different because we are a new creation with God living in our hearts. We are not going to act, talk, spend money or time the way others do simply because we are different and set apart unto the Lord. This can be challenging at times in life and especially when it comes to parenting. We are not going to parent like others as we have God living in our hearts and directing us. And while our children will be blessed with godly parents, they will also not get to do a lot of the things other kids are allowed to do. Here are a few examples from the Joiner home.

Video Games

My son may say, "Mom, my friends get to play this game. Why can't I?"

I say, "Let me see it." Then he shows me a few minutes of the video game they want to be allowed to purchase and play on their iPad. If it has real guns shooting real people, the answer is a big, "No."

"But so and so's mom allows him to play this game," he whines.

"I understand this-but I am *your* mom. God wanted me to be *your* mom. He wants me to guide you. We are not that family. We live differently."

"But why can't I play it?" he persists.

"Because I am uncomfortable with your sweet mind being corrupted by violence and death in the actions, in the weapons, and in the music of this game."

Movies

"Mom, can I watch this movie? My friends are talking about it at school."

When it comes to movies, I quickly look it up on Common Sense Media. This is a website that gives reviews on all movies current and older. It documents everything questionable in each movie, and parents can decide for themselves if they think a particular movie is something age appropriate for their children.

When reviewing what Common Sense Media says about a particular movie in question, and I read there are people using God's name in vain, or sexual acts, or violence, etc. I will say, "No my love, this movie has scenes and words I am not comfortable with you watching."

"But my friends are my same age, and they are watching it," he begs.

I may reply, "I understand their parents are allowing them to watch this. I disagree with that, but I am not their mom. I am *yours*."

As a side note, here in the Joiner home we watch PG movies. If it is PG-13, I look it up on Common Sense Media and see why and make the decision. We will never watch Rated R movies as a family as I personally have not seen one since I was 18. If I don't pollute my mind with them, I will certainly will not be allowing my kids to either.

Sleepovers

I did not allow sleepovers until my sons were in junior high and with this privilege came a long list of my standards with movies, games, electronics. I share these expectations with the other mom before the sleepover can happen. There were literal tears shed over this decision to wait until junior high for sleepovers. I am pretty sure my sons thought I was the strictest mom in the entire world. However, I have heard too many sad, compromising situations children were put in when having sleepovers too young and was simply not comfortable with this until they were older.

Vacations

When you consider vacations, think through what could benefit your children spiritually. For example, I know a family that prioritizes mission trips before other trips. Each year, they decide based on the ages of their children and where they could go to serve and shine the light of Christ. A few years ago, I strongly desired to take my children to the Ark Encounter and the Creation Museum located in northern Kentucky. The amazing life-sized Noah's Ark will take your breath away. My next goal is to take my sons to the Museum of the Bible in Washington, D.C. So even when it comes to travel, your vacations may look different from another family because you are different. You are a family of Christ followers. Your main objective is pointing your children to Christ and investing in them spiritually.

Lori, Josh and Jake in front of the life-size ark.

Our Bodies

It is important that we teach our children how precious their bodies are. I have taught my sons that their body is a gift from God. The hair color, eye color, smarts and the personality are handpicked by God and match the destiny God has planned for them. I have explained how their height will open doors for them and may close others. Their intelligence may open some doors and close others. They know God has created them on purpose, and He knows what he is doing.

I have sometimes followed this up with what the Bible has to say about our bodies in

1 Corinthians 6:18-20—

> [18] Flee from sexual immorality. All other sins a person commits are outside the body, but whoever sins sexually, sins against their own body. [19] Do you not know that your bodies are temples of the Holy Spirit, who is in you, whom you have received from God? You are not your own; [20] you were bought at a price. Therefore, honor God with your bodies.

The Corinthian society had a mindset which tended to divide body and soul. They saw the body as temporal. To them, gluttony, sexual immorality, etc., was tolerated since they felt the body did not matter that much and would eventually die and be put in the ground anyway.

Some new Corinthian believers came to think that as well. They reasoned, "God saved my soul. My body is temporal, so what's the big deal if I have sex with a temple prostitute, or fall into total gluttony, or feed any other addiction, my soul is still saved!"

Christianity, however, does not divide the body and soul. It takes very seriously the physical realm. God created the physical world; He created our physical bodies and called them good. Further, Jesus himself took on a physical body of flesh and blood and came to live with us in our physical world. He used that physical body to die for the sins of mankind. Our physical body is not something to be dismissed or abused but is precious. Paul goes on to say our body is the temple of the Holy Spirit.

In the Gotquestions.org article, "What does it mean that the body is the temple of the Holy Spirit?" It states, "If God meant simply to convey the idea that the Spirit lives within the believer, He could well have used words such as "home," "house," or "residence". But by choosing the word "temple" to describe the Spirit's dwelling, He conveys the idea that our bodies are a sacred place, in which the Spirit not only lives, but is revered and honored."

When we place our faith in God, the Holy Spirit comes to live in our lives. He is the helper directing us from the inside out according to God's plan for our lives, so we are not our own to do with our bodies whatever we want. We are God's, and we steward our bodies differently than others.

Finally, we are bought with a price. Our body and our soul were bought by Christ's death on the cross on our behalf. Not only did God create our body, but since we were what the Bible refers to a "slave to sin" we have been redeemed or bought back.

I am teaching my sons that their bodies are a gift from God. They don't get to do with it whatever they want. I explain how we are to be great stewards of our bodies and use our body to worship God. When it comes to marriage, sex, dating, even the sad transgender confusion of our day, I point back to these verses to teach my sons they are different than others. We are God's, and He has a plan for us. Our bodies are a part of that plan. Let me now unpack a few areas I talk to my sons about.

Dating

My children are not old enough to date yet. However, I have already begun to discuss what the Bible has to say about the type of person we should marry. And since we marry people we date, we should make sure we date people who are also Christ followers. We need to start this conversation before they reach the dating age.

2 Corinthians 6:14 "Do not be yoked together with unbelievers. For what do righteousness and wickedness have in common? Or what fellowship can light have with darkness?"

Driving down the road just three days ago, I brought this verse to my sons ages 12 and 14. I explained a yoke was used to tie two oxen together to plow a field. If a weak ox was tied to a strong ox, they would not pull correctly or in a straight line, one would hold back the other. I taught them how God wants us to marry a spouse who loves Him and wants to serve Him. I explained since we are Christ followers, we are different. We follow God's advice the best we can.

We talked through some sad scenarios which would arise if they made a different choice and married a person who was not a Christ follower. Sad scenarios such as their future children possibly not knowing God, not trusting in Christ and a host of other sad issues. I remind them often that who they date matters as that is who we end up marrying, eventually. I told them that they were not allowed to date anyone who was not a believer in Jesus Christ and how I would not be a good mommy if I taught them any differently. I also encouraged them that I was praying for them. Praying God would bring amazing, godly, beautiful women into their lives to be a great mate for them.

Sex

I have told my children numerous times that sex is a gift from God to enjoy on their wedding night. I explained to them how mommy and daddy waited to have sex with each other until we were married and how it was my hope for them to follow this example as well. I have also explained the many sad consequences if they choose not to wait, such as comparing their spouse with past people, sexually transmitted diseases and unwanted pregnancies. I have told them that while other kids will not follow this advice, that they are different.

1 Corinthians 6:18-20 "Flee from sexual immorality. All other sins a person commits are outside the body, but whoever sins sexually, sins against their own body."

I always point back to the Bible as my guide. God wants us to wait until marriage to have sex as He wants to protect and provide for us. Protect our mind from comparison and provide a future with a spouse without thinking of others. Protect our bodies from disease and provide a pure body to enjoy with our spouse in our future marriage. Protect from unwanted pregnancies and provide a future without regrets.

I understand I cannot control them in each of the areas I have mentioned above. There will be a time they are graduated, living on their own, and making their own choices. But I have lived some of the regrets I just outlined, and I would be a terrible, ungodly parent if I did not warn them and teach them from scripture how God's way is best.

Transgender Confusion

God tells us who we are by the body He has put us in. God made two types of humans.

Genesis 1:27 "So God created mankind in his own image, in the image of God he created them; male and female he created them."

My soul was put in a female body and therefore, it is God's plan for my life to be a female. Since my time on earth is brief compared to eternity, I need to use this body to lay us as much treasure in heaven as possible while I am here. While others may look at how they feel, what a psychologist suggests, or what may be trending currently, I do not. I am different. As I quoted earlier in this chapter, God says I am "set apart", and He does not want me to act or behave or even believe as those around me do. My sons have been taught that God makes us either male or female, and we are to serve Him in those bodies for the brief time we are on this planet.

For more on this topic, may I suggest the book *When Harry Became Sally: Responding to the Transgender Moment*, by Ryan T. Anderson.

In General

When my sons complain about video games, movies or any number of issues, I will often reply by saying, "Well, take it up with God, son. He made you, *my* son. Out of all the mommies in the world, He decided you were best with me as your mom. And I am thrilled to be your mom, and we are different."

Sometimes I say, "I have been given a job to do by God, to raise you unto the Lord. I will be held accountable for the parenting job I did with you. I am not perfect. I get things wrong by yelling too much at times. Also, perhaps I'm too strict, but I am doing my best and want to hear God say, "Well done" to me when it comes to parenting you. I love you so much and want the best for you. However, the best means saying no or wait on an activity you want to do. You can know it is always out of my deep love for you and my desire to be a good steward of your life."

It is at this point I am glad I have two sons. I can't imagine the turmoil I would go through with daughters and clothes. Oh, my! My heart goes out to you, moms of daughters!

Mom and Dad, are you personally ok with being different? Are you "set apart" as God exhorted the Israelites to be in the Old Testament? Are you different from others? It will be hard for you to tell your kids they will need to be different, and you are not yourself. Perhaps point out to your kids in age-appropriate ways how you are not going along with the crowd in numerous ways. How you are a fish swimming against the tide at times because you would rather be a God pleaser than just blend in with the crowd.

The Bottom Line

We are to shine the light of Christ in and through our lives. We will stand out, for God, for righteousness and for love and kindness. We are the Spirit-filled people of God, prepared to pray for others, invite others to church and share the hope we have in Christ. As we are raising our children unto the Lord, we will be different because of this and so will our kids, and we need to teach them to embrace this early.

Chapter 12

Teach Your Children the Two Paths in Life

GOD has clearly taught all through scripture of two diverging paths. Every person on this earth must choose one. God gives no middle ground. There are two paths and two paths only. As we raise our children unto the Lord, we need to teach them about these two paths and remind them that one is of the Lord and the other is of the world.

The Bible teaches there are two paths in life.

I am going to take us on a little journey to unpack this concept. Just hang with me and absorb what the scriptures have to say, then we will apply this to parenting our children.

In Deuteronomy 30:15, God, when speaking to the Israelite people said, "See, I set before you today life and prosperity, death and destruction."

Here, we see the two paths are either life and prosperity or death and destruction.

Deuteronomy 30:19 says, "This day I call the heavens and the earth as witnesses against you that I have set before you life and death, blessings and curses. Choose life…"

Here the paths are described as life and blessings or death and curses.

Psalm 1:1-6

"1 Blessed is the one who does not walk in step with the wicked or stand in the way that sinners take or sit in the company of mockers, 2 but whose delight is in the law of the Lord, and who meditates on his law day and night. 3 That person is like a tree planted by streams of water, which yields its fruit in season and whose leaf does not wither—whatever they do prospers.4 Not so the wicked! They are like chaff that the wind blows away. 5 Therefore the wicked will not stand in the judgment, nor sinners in the assembly of the righteous. 6 For the Lord watches over the way of the righteous, but the way of the wicked leads to destruction."

These verses indicate that one path is walking in step with wicked people and mockers. Choosing this path leads to being like chaff in the wind, not standing with the righteous on the day of Judgment, and ultimately, this path ends in destruction.

The other path is with those who delight in God's laws and meditate on God's Word. Choosing this path will lead to a fruitful life, standing with the righteous on Judgment Day and having God watch over your life.

In Jeremiah 21:8, God says, "Furthermore, tell the people, 'This is what the Lord says: See, I am setting before you the way of life and the way of death.'"

These verses from scripture help put together this picture of two paths in life. Now, let's turn to the New Testament and see Jesus' teaching on this subject.

In Mathew 7:13-14, we come to Jesus' teaching on the narrow and wide gates.

"[13] Enter through the narrow gate. For wide is the gate and broad is the road that leads to destruction, and many enter through it. [14] But small is the gate and narrow the road that leads to life, and only a few find it."

Here we have Jesus teaching the multitudes during his famous Sermon on the Mount, describing narrow and wide gates and narrow and broad roads. One gate and road leads to destruction, death and hell. The other gate and road leads to life.

The narrow gate, or Luke calls it a door, is talking about salvation. Recall Jesus called Himself the gate. John 10:9 says, "I am the gate; whoever enters through me will be saved." He is the narrow way of salvation. Faith in Jesus Christ as Savior is the only option for eternal life with Him in heaven. Once you place your faith in Christ, the narrow gate, you are to stay on and continually choose the narrow road.

In Luke 6, we can read of two types of builders-one building on sand and one building on rock. In Ezekiel chapter 11, God exhorts his people have an undivided heart-to choose one path, the righteous path, and stick to it. In the book of Revelation, Jesus says He does not want lukewarm followers, and when we are lukewarm, not choosing one path or the other, it makes Him want to vomit.

All through scripture, we are continually confronted with two ways to live, two paths to follow. There is no middle ground.

Steps to point your children along the narrow path:

We must be clear about the two paths. All through their lives, our children will have opportunities to choose the narrow path, and they will most likely be in the minority when choosing to follow God in righteous living. The narrow path is the unpopular path, but we and our children need to follow it.

1. **Teach your children the two paths.**

I have taught this to my sons in varying degrees all their lives. They have been taught from scripture, by me, and by church leaders about building their house on the solid rock of Jesus Christ, not the shaking ground of the shifting, confused culture we live in today.

We need to place our faith in Christ and build our lives, seeking His will at each turn. Not placing our faith in Christ is shaky ground, like sand in a storm. It is not stable and will not help us in life or eternity. Josh and Jake could 100% recite these Bible teachings at ages 11 and 13. They could have done it much earlier. So that is step one, to teach the Bible stories and verses I have just shared in this chapter.

2. **Remind them of the two paths throughout their lives.**

I may say driving in the car, "Boys, God is clear in scripture that there are two paths in life. Do you recall what those paths are? What are examples of people in your junior high choosing the wide path? What are examples of kids choosing the narrow path?" I may have this conversation while I am driving or perhaps while I am fixing lunch or after school while they are telling me stories about their day. I try to connect their story of a situation with this biblical teaching.

As they get older and perhaps have a tricky decision to make, I will say, "Son, I hope you choose life and the narrow road." Or "Everyone has a choice. They can choose the road leading to destruction or the road leading to life. Which do you think you need to choose in this situation?"

Alan walking boys into church.

3. Reiterate this teaching through prayer.

When I pray for my children, I pray for this specifically. I may say, "Oh Lord, please keep Josh on the narrow path today. Please help him stand strong in temptation and not choose a path that would lead to destruction." Or "Thank you Lord that Jake is yours. He is your sheep. He hears your voice, and you empower him to build a fruitful life in you, his solid rock of salvation!" Or even, "Oh Lord, I pray today that if everyone is choosing the easy path, the wide path, you would give Josh and Jake the leadership, the fortitude and the perseverance to follow you in righteous living even if they follow you alone."

The Bottom Line

Teaching biblical stories and parables to your children is step one. Then help them to apply this teaching to life as you ask them questions and pray over them comes next. The Bible is clear about two paths, and I encourage you to teach your children clearly the two paths and choose righteousness yourself.

We must say to our children, "There are two paths in life. I want you to choose God's way. I am praying for you and raising you to be able to choose God, even when it is tough. His way leads to a life of fruitfulness. His way leads to Him watching over you. His way leads to you standing with the righteous on Judgment Day. You will have to choose, and I pray you choose life!"

Chapter 13

Prayer, Repetition and Encouragement

AS we come to the final chapter, I want to share a few final insights with you as you are raising your children unto the Lord. In chapter one, I shared at length how important it was to pray for your children out loud each day and why you should do this on multiple levels. Here, I will share a few more items I pray for my sons on a regular basis. You can use them as well to pray for your kids.

My children's future spouse

I regularly pray for my sons' future spouse in front of them. "Oh Lord, I pray you would bring a godly wife into Josh's life. That she would be a God-fearing woman who loves you with her whole heart."

My children's friends

I pray for my sons' friends in front of them, "Oh Lord, would bring godly men and women into Jake's life to always point him to you. I pray their friends would be godly influences on them, and they would be godly influences on others."

My children's future career

I pray for their future careers in front of them. "Oh Lord, I pray Josh and Jake would know their calling in life early and be able to have focus in their lives. I pray you put them in situations where they can expand and grow the God-given gifts and talents you have placed in them. I pray for divine appointments and open doors to great careers where they can provide for their families as well as have a significant influence for you. Please grant them a close walk with you to be able to experience all the good works you prepared in advance for them to walk in. I pray everything they do would prosper, succeed for their benefit and for your glory."

My grandchildren

I even pray for my future grandchildren in front of them. Deuteronomy 5:10 says, "God lavishes his love on those who love him and obey his commands even for a thousand generations." So, I pray, "Oh Lord, I pray Josh and Jake would walk with you, love you with their whole heart and obey your commands, so my grandchildren, their children and grandchildren could be lavished with your love and blessings for a thousand generations."

I encourage you to keep praying for your kids out loud, every day. Ask God to give you wisdom and insight as to what to pray, and feel free to use what I say as a guide in the meantime.

Repetition is key in prayer and Bible teaching.

Repetition is a good thing. You are explaining biblical concepts to your kids weekly, monthly and yearly, in an ongoing way, and this is key. Don't give up. For example, I pray regularly for my sons to live long lives and lay up much treasure in Heaven for God's glory. I typically do this when I am waking my children up each day. For me, I need to continue repetition in this area as I cannot guarantee they even heard me the first 5 times I prayed! They may not have been awake!

It is OK to have items you are regularly praying for your children over and over. When my sons were in preschool, I was praying for them to be protected and to come home safe to their pillows. When my sons were in elementary, I prayed the same thing daily. Now that they are in junior high, the same thing. What do you think I will be praying for them in high school and college? You guessed it! That each night they would lay their head on their pillow in safety, abundant health and peace.

Even if they don't grasp what I was praying for them, they will remember their mom and dad prayed over them, covering them with prayers and asking God to protect and guide them. They will remember their parents prayed they would be filled with the Holy Spirit, covered with the blood of Christ and delivered home safely each night.

Therefore, please embrace repetition. It is ok, and not just with our prayers, but with our teachings as well. I am teaching my sons how to have an eternal perspective at each age and each stage. They may not be fully grasping it now; however, over time, it will sink in.

Two weeks ago, I drove my boys to see my dad in East Texas. We passed by a cemetery. I said, "Boys, do you see that cemetery? All those people had one shot each! One shot to live for God and to walk into the good works He had prepared in advance for them to do. One shot to live for Christ and further the Great Commission. Their turn is over, but we still have ours. You have one shot to be God's man in this generation, one shot to live a life of shining your light for Christ." When they are older and pass by a cemetery, I want them to be reminded of this basic truth, so I am laying the groundwork now while they are young and in my care. I am teaching them this truth multiple times.

I have taught them to have an eternal perspective for years, but why not double click on that when I can? I promise you, passing by that cemetery won't be the last time I remind them that an eternal perspective is better than a temporal one.

Your children are your main and most important disciples.

Never forget our children are our main disciples. The Bible puts their spiritual development in *our* hands. Don't leave this up to someone at church. Never assume they will just pick up these lessons along the way. It does not have to be fancy. We just need to be intentional.

You could simply teach them what you are reading in the Bible. When my boys wake up early, they come upstairs and see me sitting at my desk reading my Bible. Josh, my 14-year-old, came upstairs, and I said, "Josh, I was just reading in Deuteronomy about how blessed the Israelite people were, and that is what I hope for you, my son! That God would be with you and bless you!"

Taking ownership of your child's spiritual development does not have to be scary or complicated. It does not have to take a ton of time. Consistency will be key. It does not have to be overwhelming. Remember, you can put a few items in place. Then, things will be on autopilot! You can do it!

Josh reading his Bible outside.

Put the basics in place.

1. Pray for your kids each day, out loud. Pray for them the things you would hope someone would pray for you.
2. Read the Bible, teach your children and grandchildren what you are reading.
3. Plug into a church with a solid biblically based children's ministry. Volunteer in the kid's ministry, so you know what is being taught and can remind your children during the week.

4. Go to a Christian bookstore or look online for Christian resources, buy them and read to your kids.

The Bottom Line

Don't be intimated by not having enough time or not knowing enough. You have God on your side, leading and directing you. Keep praying for your kids out loud. Keep teaching basic Bible lessons and continue praying the same prayers. Use car time, breakfast time and waking up in the morning to point your kids to the Lord. You can do this, and I am always here to help!

I am rooting for you! I hope this book has been an encouragement and gives you practical tools to raise your children unto the Lord! If you have been particularly touched by one of the chapters, I would love to hear from you. You are welcome to reach out to me on my website at LoriJoinerMinistries.org and click the "contact Lori" tab and send me a note!

About Lori Joiner

LORI Joiner is a sought-after speaker, author and discipleship coach. She is the author of *Discipling Women, Start Here Six Foundational Lessons for Growth in Christ, Next Steps Seven Foundational Lessons for Growth in Christ* and *The Discipleship Starter Kit.*

She traveled nationally and internationally as a full-time missionary with Cru, formerly Campus Crusade for Christ, for 22 years gaining extensive experience in cross-cultural ministry, evangelism, discipleship and directing women's ministries.

She has lived overseas, undercover sharing the love of Jesus in several closed countries.

Lori founded and directed the Faith House, a discipleship home for college-aged women in Waco, Texas.

She is the founder of Lori Joiner Ministries, which serves the global body of Christ with discipleship resources, publications, ongoing coaching and consulting of discipleship ministries.

Lori travels extensively teaching on a wide variety of topics and currently makes her home in Katy, TX, with her husband Alan and two sons, Josh and Jake.

Lori has a weekly podcast called *Your Discipleship Coach* available on Apple Podcast, Spotify and her website under the podcast tab.

To see a full list of her resources or to bring her to speak at your next retreat, event or discipleship training, you can find her at LoriJoinerMinistries.org.

Made in the USA
Columbia, SC
31 October 2022